P9-DVO-917

To

- -

From

- -

- -

For Callie and Simon. You're never too old to read these stories again   S. J. D.

Published by Lion Children's Books
an imprint of
Lion Hudson plc
Wilkinson House, Jordan Hill Road,
Oxford OX2 8DR, England
www.lionhudson.com/lionchildrens

ISBN 978 0 7459 6303 7

First edition 2015

Acknowledgments
The Bible retellings are based on the corresponding passages from the Good News Bible © 1994 published by the Bible Societies/HarperCollins Publishers Ltd UK, Good News Bible© American Bible Society 1966, 1971, 1976, 1992. Used with permission.

A catalogue record for this book is available from the British Library

Printed and bound in China, January 2015, LH41

The Lion
PICTURE BIBLE

Retold by Sarah J. Dodd
Illustrated by Raffaella Ligi

LI♥N
CHILDREN'S

Contents
The Old Testament

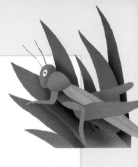

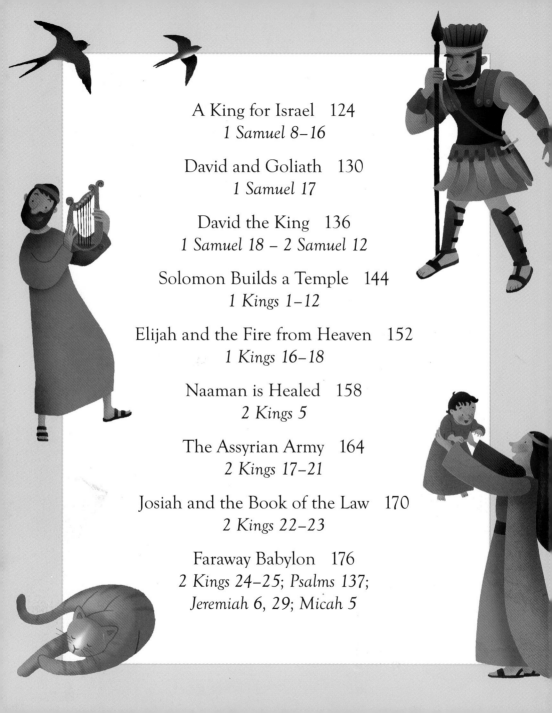

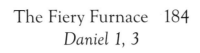

The New Testament

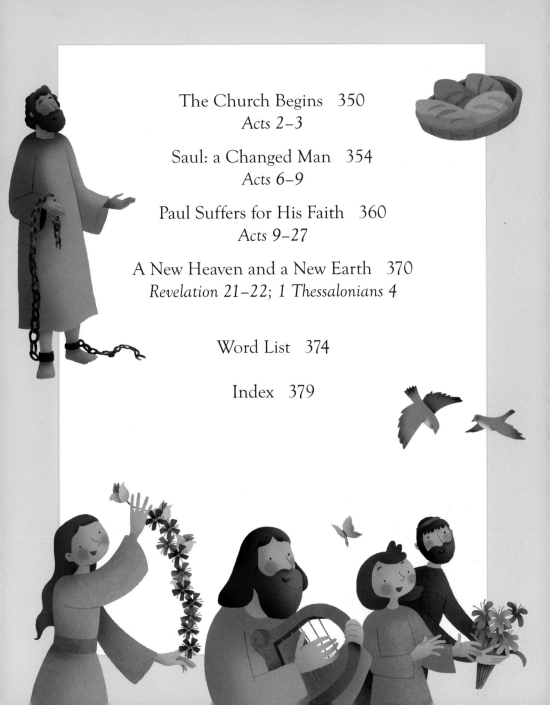

THE OLD TESTAMENT

In the Beginning

Long before time began, there was no earth. Just swirling, watery darkness with nothing in it.

But God was there.

God spoke: "Let there be light!"

Dazzling light appeared for the first time, chasing away the darkness.

"This is the first day ever," said God.

The darkness came back for a while, and God called it night. But next morning the light returned, as it always would.

On the second day, God said, "Let there be sky!"

The sky unrolled, stretching out and spreading blankets of soft cloud.

"This is a good thing," God said. "Now I will separate the dry land from the sea."

Volcanoes erupted and mountains folded into shape. There was plenty of land, but nothing lived on it.

A vast ocean filled the rest of the planet, sparkling in the fresh, new light. But nothing lived in it; the water was empty and quiet.

Another night came and went. When dawn broke, God said, "I'm going to make plants, but they need sunshine to grow."

The sun exploded into life and warmed the earth.

Lush grass sprang up, and trees that were heavy with fruit and seeds.

Out in space, God made the moon and stars to light the sky so that it was never completely dark, even at night.

God saw that the world was wonderful. But it was not finished yet.

God filled the seas with every kind of
swimming, darting creature; God sent soaring,
fluttering birds to throng the sky. They sang
and squawked, trilling their music across the
earth.

Animals, wild and tame, galloped and leapt,
wriggled and slept on the beautiful earth God
had made for them.

God saw that the
world was amazing.
But still there was
something missing.
So God made the first
people – a man called Adam
and a woman called Eve.
"You will be my special friends," said
God. "This earth I have made provides all
that you need. You must take care of it."
God had finished his work. It was time to
rest.
"This world and everything in it is very
good," said God. "It's very good indeed!"

The Garden of Eden

God planted a beautiful garden, called Eden, for Adam and Eve to live in.

"Everything in this garden is for you," said God, "but you must not eat from the tree in the middle of the garden. If you do, death will come into the world."

One day, the sly snake slithered up to Eve and whispered in her ear.

"Why not eat from that tree in the middle?" it hissed.

"Oh, no," said Eve. "God says that if we eat from it, we will die."

The snake flickered its forked tongue. "You won't die; you will become as wise as God!"

Eve looked at the tree. The fruit did look tempting…

Eve took some of the fruit and bit into it.

"It *is* delicious," she said, and she handed a piece to Adam, who took a bite as well.

Adam smacked his lips. "That tastes good!" he said with a smile.

But their smiles didn't last long. They knew they had done wrong.

When God came to the garden in the evening, Adam and Eve hid.

"Come out," said God, sadly. "You didn't trust me. Now you must leave the garden. Otherwise you might eat from my special Tree of Life. Then you will live for ever, and so will the wrong things you have done.

"You will have to work hard to grow your own food; it will be difficult and lonely. You have broken our friendship."

Adam and Eve felt so ashamed that they even wanted to hide their bodies from God, who had made them. God gave them some clothes to wear and sent them out of the garden.

"What have
we done?"
said Adam,
poking gloomily at
the hard, bare soil.
"Look," Eve said,
pointing back at the
beautiful garden.
An angel with a flaming
sword was guarding the way to
the Tree of Life.
"There's no way back," said Adam.
"Our children will have to live out
here, too."

"I'm hungry," said Eve. It was a new feeling.

They sighed, shook their heads, and began to dig.

And Adam was right. When their children were born, they too had to join in with the hard work to produce food. Life would never be easy again.

Noah and the Flood

Adam and Eve had children and grandchildren. The human family grew until there were lots of people on the earth. They did bad things to one another and ignored God. God was sorry that he had ever made any people at all. But there was one good man, whose name was Noah. God decided that he would help Noah and his family to make a fresh start on the earth. "I want you to make an ark," God said to Noah; "a special, safe place to keep something precious."

"An ark? Do you mean some kind of box?" asked Noah.

"This ark will be a boat," said God. "I will tell you exactly how long, wide, and tall it must be."

Noah listened carefully. The boat was going to be enormous!

"Why would I need such a huge boat?" he gasped. "My family is only small, and the land is dry. This boat won't float!"

"I will send rain," said God. "A flood will cover everything on the earth, except you, your family, and the animals in the ark."

"Animals?" For a moment Noah looked puzzled. "Oh, of course. I guess we'll need one or two goats for milk, and some chickens for eggs."

"I want you to take two of every kind of animal," said God. "Take a male and a female, so that they can have babies when the land is dry again. And you can take more of your precious flocks."

Noah set to work. He did everything exactly as God had commanded, and the last of the animals hurried into the boat just as the rain began to pour.

Noah checked that everyone was aboard, and God shut the door behind them.

It rained and rained. Houses and fields disappeared beneath the water; trees vanished too. The flood rose so high that even the highest mountaintops became tiny islands and then they were gone.

After forty days, the rain stopped, but the land was still covered in water.

One day there was a sudden BUMP.

"We've hit something," said Noah. "But I can't see what it is."

There was nothing to do but wait. One day a small piece of land appeared beneath the ark.

"The water has gone down a little!" said Noah. Everyone shouted for joy.

Noah sent a raven flying out over the flood. It flew back and forth, looking for somewhere to nest, but it didn't come back.

"I wonder if there is more dry land somewhere?" said Noah.

So Noah sent a dove flying out over the water, but there was nowhere nearby to land, so it came back. A week later, he sent it out again. This time, it came back with a leafy olive twig in its beak.

"There must be trees not too far away," said Noah, "and they've been above water long enough to start growing again."

At last, the flood cleared, and the animals stepped off the ark. The air was noisy with the sound of bleats and barks, grunts and growls.

"I'm making a new promise to you and all the people after you," said God. "I will never flood the whole earth again."

The first rainbow appeared, arching across the sky.

"Whenever you see a rainbow, remember my promise," said God. "This is a new beginning for the world."

The Tower of Babel

"What's this thing?" The workman picked up a
strange object that looked like a stone but had
straight edges. "Oof! It's heavy!"

"It's called a brick," the builder explained.
"Now we've worked out how to make these,
we can build amazing things."

"Like what?"

"Taller buildings, bigger cities." The builder

looked around at the bustling streets. "Things are getting so crowded. We need homes for everyone."

The city leaders were passing by and heard the builder's words.

"We're going to build a wonderful city," they said, "with a tower tall enough to spear the sky. Nothing like it has been done before. We'll be famous!"

God watched as the tower grew.

"These people are too proud of themselves," said God. "They need to learn a lesson. I will make them speak in different languages."

"Keep laying the bricks!" said the builder.

"What did you say?" The workman put down his tools. "*Flobbidifibbetigumble*?"

"Stop talking nonsense and get on with your work," snapped the builder.

"Why are you talking all funny?"

"Speak properly!"

The builder poked the workman in the shoulder; the workman whacked the builder with his hammer.

Everyone began to fight, babbling angrily in different languages. In the end, they quarrelled so badly that they didn't even want to live near each other. They went to live in separate places.

The tower was never finished. It stood alone, pointing up to heaven like a broken finger.

Abraham and His Family

"Abram, I want you to leave your home," said God.

"What?" Abram looked up from shearing a sheep. "Why? Where shall I go?"

"I'll show you," said God. "I just want you to make a start."

Abram called his wife, Sarai. They took with them everything they owned and set off.

Abram didn't know where they were going, but he trusted that God would show him.

Sure enough, when they reached a great oak tree in the land of Canaan, God said, "This is the country where you are to live. I will give it as a gift to your children."

"I haven't got any children," said Abram. "Sarai and I would love to have some, but we're getting too old."

"Look at the dust in your sandals," whispered God. "Can you count how many specks there are? That's how many people will be in your family. I'm going to change your names to Abraham and Sarah. The new names will remind you of my new promise."

Abraham smiled and wiggled his dusty toes.

Abraham and Sarah set up campx and settled in the land that God had given them.

One day, three strangers came into the camp.

"We must be kind to these people," said Abraham. "Sarah, prepare some food and drink for them."

As the visitors ate, one of them said a curious thing: "I will come back this time next year, and by then you will have a son."

Abraham knew then that these people were messengers from God. The promise was going to come true!

But Sarah laughed.

"There's no way an old woman like me can have a baby!" she said. "It's impossible."

A year later, Sarah was laughing for a different reason. She and Abraham were full of joy as they held their baby boy in their arms.

"Our son's name shall be Isaac," declared Abraham.

Sarah nodded, and her old eyes crinkled as she rocked the baby. "God has kept his promise," she said.

Jacob and Esau

Isaac watched as the camels appeared out of the dusty desert. A young woman was riding one of them. Her name was Rebecca and she was Isaac's relative. She had left her father and her brother Laban, and had come to be Isaac's wife.

"You've had a long journey," Isaac said as he greeted her. "You must be tired."

Rebecca smiled and bowed her head, and Isaac knew that he would love her.

They married, and Rebecca gave birth to twin boys: Jacob and Esau.

As the boys grew, each of their parents loved one better than the other. Isaac preferred Esau, a hairy man who liked to be outdoors and was a great hunter.

Rebecca's favourite was smooth-skinned Jacob, who liked to sit quietly in the tents and talk with her.

Isaac grew old and almost blind. He knew that
he was going to die soon, so he called for Esau.

"You are my eldest son," he said. "Take your
weapons and go out hunting. Prepare a meal
in the tasty way I like; then I will give you a
special blessing."

Esau nodded and went out.

"Jacob!" hissed Rebecca. "I want you to have that blessing instead, so let's play a trick. Go and fetch a couple of goats and I will make a delicious stew. Then I'll dress you up like Esau, with goatskins to make your arms hairy like his. You can take the stew to your father and he will bless you instead of your brother!"

Jacob went to his father, Isaac. "It's me," he said. "I'm your son, Esau.

"I've brought the stew, Father, just as you asked. Now give me your blessing."

"You came back quickly," said Isaac, suspiciously. "And you sound different. Are you really Esau?"

"Of course I am," lied Jacob.

Isaac blessed Jacob and said a special prayer for him. Jacob left, smiling about his trick.

A few moments later, Esau came in with a stew for his father.

"Here I am," he said. "You can give me your blessing now."

"What?" cried Isaac. "If you are Esau, who was here before?"

They realized that they had been tricked. Esau was furious and vowed that one day he would get his own back on his lying brother, Jacob.

Jacob Learns a Lesson

"Run away, Jacob!" said Rebecca. "Esau is so angry that he wants to kill you! Go to my brother, your Uncle Laban."

So Jacob left. That night he had to sleep outdoors, using a rock for a pillow.

While he slept, Jacob dreamed of a stairway between earth and heaven, with angels going up and down it. God stood above him and repeated the promise he had given to Jacob's grandfather, Abraham:

"This land where you lie belongs to you and your family," said God. "Wherever you go, I will watch over you and I will bring you back here in the end."

When Jacob awoke, he took the rock and set it up as a marker to show where he had seen God.

Then he journeyed on to Laban's house.
He offered to look after the sheep.

"I'll work for seven years if you let me marry
your daughter Rachel," he said.

"It's a deal," said Laban.

So Jacob worked hard for seven years, but the
time passed quickly because he loved Rachel so
much.

After the wedding, Jacob lifted his wife's veil and fell back in shock.

"It's not Rachel!" he shouted. "It's her elder sister, Leah. Uncle Laban, you've tricked me!"

Laban shrugged. "It's a tradition that the older daughter should marry first. Work for me another seven years and you shall have Rachel too."

Jacob had to agree. For seven years, he took care of Laban's animals. But it was worth it, because Rachel also became his wife, and their marriage was as happy as Jacob had hoped.

As the years passed, Jacob had many children of his own. "It's time to go back home to Canaan," he said.

"Stay a while longer," said Laban. "I must pay you for your work."

"All right," said Jacob. "Let me have all your animals with dark or spotty coats."

Laban agreed, but then he hid all the animals with dark or spotty coats, so that Jacob would have none! He had forgotten that Jacob was as

clever as he was – God gave Jacob the wisdom to breed the animals carefully. He made sure that all the strongest animals had new babies with dark or spotty coats. God helped him with this, and Jacob's flocks grew until he became very wealthy.

God told Jacob that it was time to go back to his home in Canaan. So he took his family and everything he owned, and set off.

But as Jacob got closer to Canaan, he began to worry. He remembered Esau's threats and sent messengers ahead to find out where his brother might be.

At last a messenger returned with some news. "Esau is coming, with 400 men!" he cried.

Jacob began to shiver and shake.

"What if Esau still wants to kill me?" he said. "I'd better send him a present."

Jacob's servants went ahead with sheep and goats, cows, camels, and donkeys. Jacob waited, worried, and waited some more.

At last, he saw Esau and his men coming. He looked around. There was no time to run away.

Instead, he bowed down and waited to be killed.

But Esau raced over and hugged him.

"Let's forget all the bad things in the past," he said. "I want to be your loving brother again."

Joseph and His Brothers

Jacob had twelve sons, but he loved Joseph and Benjamin best of all. They were the two sons that Rachel had borne. Jacob made Joseph a beautiful coat to show how precious he was. This gave Joseph big ideas about himself.

"I had a strange dream," Joseph told his family. "We were tying up sheaves of wheat in the field, and my tall sheaf stood in the middle while yours bowed down to it."

"If you think we're going to bow down to you, you're wrong," growled the brothers.

Joseph went on. "Another time I dreamed that the sun, the moon, and eleven stars were all bowing down to me!"

Jacob was furious. "Who do you think you are?" he said.

The brothers were glad to get away and take the goats to find good grass. But Jacob sent Joseph to check on them.

"Let's kill him!" they snarled.

"No!" said the eldest brother, Reuben. "We can throw him into this dried-up well instead."

So the brothers ripped Joseph's coat off and threw him in the well. Reuben, thinking that Joseph was safe, went to check on the goats.

But while Reuben was away, some merchants came by with their camels, carrying spices to sell in Egypt.

"We have something you can sell!" laughed Judah. He and his brothers handed Joseph over for twenty pieces of silver.

When Reuben returned, he was horrified to see that Joseph had gone. "What shall I tell Father now?" he wailed.

"We'll roll Joseph's coat in goat's blood," said Judah. "We can say that a wild animal killed him."

So the brothers went home to break the news to Jacob, while Joseph was carried away to Egypt.

Joseph in Egypt

The traders sold Joseph in Egypt's slave market.
A wealthy man bought him and treated him
well.

However, his master's wife told lies to get
him into trouble. He was thrown into jail.

"You think your story's bad?" said one of the
other prisoners. "I used to be the wine servant

in the palace of Pharaoh, the king of Egypt, before I got thrown in here. And now I'm worried about a strange dream."

"What happened?" asked Joseph.

"I picked some grapes from a vine with three branches and squeezed them into Pharaoh's cup. What does it mean?"

Joseph prayed, asking God to tell him the answer.

"Don't worry," he said. "In three days, Pharaoh will take you back to be his servant."

"I had a dream too!" said another prisoner. "I used to be Pharaoh's baker, and in the dream I was carrying three baskets on my head, full of pastries for Pharaoh. But the birds ate them all up."

Joseph's face grew sad. "In three days, you too will leave prison. But Pharaoh will kill you."

Everything happened just as Joseph had said.
So when Pharaoh himself had frightening
dreams, he called Joseph to the palace.

"In my dreams, seven thin cows ate seven
fat cows," said Pharaoh, "and seven dry ears
of grain gobbled up seven healthy ones. What
does this mean?"

"God is warning you," said Joseph. "For
seven years, there will be good harvests and
plenty to eat. Then there will be seven years
when the crops fail and there will be no food."

"What shall I do?" cried Pharaoh.

"Choose someone to take charge of the food and store part of the crop during the good years," said Joseph. "Then there will be enough to eat during the bad years."

"You're sensible," declared Pharaoh. "*You* can do it!"

So Joseph did exactly that. He became the second most important person in all Egypt.

One day, ten men arrived from Canaan,
starving and thin.

"Please give us some grain," they begged.
Joseph recognized his brothers, but they
didn't know who he was. Benjamin was not
with them, and Joseph longed to see him.

"Bring your youngest brother, too," Joseph said. "Then you can have all the grain you want."

So the brothers trailed home again and returned with Benjamin. Joseph was overjoyed to see him.

"I can't let him go again," he thought. "How can I keep him here?"

Joseph filled the brothers' sacks with grain. Then he had an idea. As he was waving goodbye, he asked a servant to slip a silver cup into the top of Benjamin's sack.

After the brothers had left, he shouted, "My silver cup is missing!" and sent his servants to chase after them.

His servants searched through every sack until they found the cup. They brought the brothers back to Egypt and told Joseph where the cup had been found.

"So Benjamin is the thief!" roared Joseph. "He must pay for this. He will be my slave from now on."

"No!" the brothers begged. "Our father lost his son Joseph a long time ago. He will die of sadness if he loses Benjamin too."

Joseph couldn't keep his secret any longer. "*I* am Joseph," he declared.

When the brothers realized that he was telling the truth, they raced back to Canaan to tell Jacob the good news. The whole family packed up and moved to Egypt.

Joseph hugged Jacob.

"God has used me to save your lives," said Joseph. "Now we are all together again."

Moses the Runaway

Many children and grandchildren were born into Joseph's family. They became a nation: the people of Israel.

"There are too many people," complained the new pharaoh. "Soon there will be more of them than there are of us!

"I know! I'll declare them my slaves. They can make bricks under the hot sun for my luxury buildings." If they stopped to rest, the Egyptian slave masters whipped them.

"Work harder!" they shouted.

But still Israel grew.

"There are more Israelites than ever," growled Pharaoh. "Kill their baby boys!"

One brave mother was determined to save her baby. She made a basket waterproof, laid her baby in it, and placed it among the reeds at the edge of the River Nile. The baby's sister, Miriam, hid close by to watch.

Pharaoh's daughter came down to the river with her servants, to cool off in the water.

"What's that noise?" she said. "It sounds like a baby crying."

She peered through the reeds and saw the basket. She sent a servant to fetch it.

"It's one of the Israelite babies!" said Pharaoh's daughter. "I shall call him Moses. I will bring him up as my son."

Miriam stepped forward.

"You will need someone to help you care for him," she said, timidly. "Shall I fetch my mother?"

Pharaoh's daughter agreed. She gave Moses back to his real mother until he was old enough to go and live in the palace.

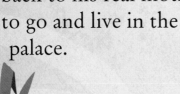

So Moses grew up as a prince. One day, he saw
an Egyptian slave master hitting an Israelite
man to make him work harder. He looked
around quickly.

"No one is watching," he thought. "I'll teach
that Egyptian a lesson."

Moses killed the Egyptian and hid his body
in the sand.

When Pharaoh discovered what had happened, he was furious.

"Moses must die too!" he roared.

Moses was frightened, so he ran away into the desert. He settled with a family there and became a shepherd.

The years passed. Moses' new life was simple but happy. But far away in Egypt, things were as bad as ever.

Then one day, something strange happened.

Moses was looking after his sheep when he noticed a bush that seemed to be on fire. Flames darted out in every direction, and yet the bush was not burning up.

He stepped closer and was startled to hear a voice calling his name.

"Moses! Moses!"

Moses gulped. "Here I am."

"I am God," said the voice, and Moses began to shiver and shake.

"I am going to rescue my people, the Israelites, from Egypt," said God. "I want you to go to Pharaoh and ask him to let them go."

Moses was more afraid than ever. "Please send someone else," he begged.

But God had chosen Moses. "Your brother Aaron will help you," he said, "and my power will do the rest."

Escape from Egypt

Moses and his brother Aaron stood before Pharaoh's throne.

"God wants you to let the Israelites go," declared Moses.

"My answer is *no*," said Pharaoh.

"Let us show you what God's power can do," said Moses.

Aaron threw his stick down. It turned into a slithering snake!

But Pharaoh's magicians stepped forward and turned their sticks into snakes as well.

"You'll have to do better than that, Moses!" sneered Pharaoh.

But Pharaoh soon discovered just how powerful God was.

First of all, the River Nile turned to blood.
Then frogs and gnats, flies and terrible diseases
came upon the Egyptians.

The Israelites stayed safe and healthy.

A dreadful hailstorm knocked the Egyptian
crops to the ground. A swarm of locusts
followed behind, nibbling and gobbling every
last scrap of food that remained.

The Israelites had enough to eat.

The whole sky turned black, and it was so dark across Egypt that nobody could see a thing.

But each time Moses went to ask Pharaoh to let the Israelites go, Pharaoh said, "*No!* I will *not* let them go."

God spoke to Moses. "Tell the Israelites to get ready, for tonight I will set them free. Every Egyptian home will suffer, for the eldest boy in each of their families is going to die. But I will save my own people."

"What must we do to get ready?" asked Moses.

"Each family must prepare bread to take on the journey," ordered God. "There's no time to let it rise, so make it without yeast. They must also eat a good meal of roast lamb and paint a bit of the blood on the door frame of their house, to show that they belong to me. When death comes, it will pass over that home. The people will be safe."

That night, death came in the darkness to all the Egyptian families.

"You can go," wept Pharaoh. "Take everything with you and leave us alone."

The Israelites were free to go.

This became known as the Passover, because death passed over the homes of God's people without harming them.

The Ten Commandments

The Israelites had escaped from Egypt, but their troubles weren't over.

When they reached the shores of the Red Sea, they looked behind and saw Egyptian soldiers and horses.

"Don't be afraid," Moses told them. "God will fight for us."

Moses held his stick out over the sea and

the waves peeled back, making two great walls
of whooshing water with a dry path between
them.

The Egyptians chased the Israelites across the
seabed. But as the last person scurried to safety,
the sea rolled back over the Egyptians and
swept them away.

"God has saved us!" sang the Israelites,
dancing for joy.

After several weeks of walking in the desert, the Israelites came to a mountain called Sinai. Thick cloud covered it, and thunder echoed off the rocks. The people trembled with fear.

God called Moses to meet him on top of the mountain. He wrote ten laws on two pieces of stone and gave them to Moses. They were special laws for his people to keep for all time:

1 I am the only God. Always put me first.
2 Don't worship anyone or anything but me.
3 Don't say you are acting in my name when you're not.
4 Rest for one day at the end of each week. Call this special day the sabbath.
5 Respect your parents.
6 Don't murder anyone.
7 Be faithful to your husband or wife.
8 Don't steal.
9 Don't lie to get other people into trouble.
10 Don't be jealous about things that other people have.

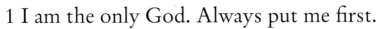

When Moses came down, he showed the laws to the Israelites.

"God has made a special promise, called a covenant, with us," he said. "He will be our God and will love and protect us. He will give us a home of our own. In return, we need to trust him and obey his commands."

The craftsmen made a special box, called an ark, to keep the two stones in. On top, they put two angels made of gold.

"We will carry the ark of the covenant with us," said Moses. "It will remind us that the real, living God is here with us."

"Who will carry it?" said Aaron.

"You and the members of your family will take special care of it. You will be called priests."

There was more work to do. The ark of the covenant was so important that it needed to be kept in its own tent.

"It's not an ordinary tent, like the ones we live in," said Moses. "It will be the place where all the people can come and worship God. It is to be called the tabernacle."

So the Israelites used all their skills and the best materials to make the tabernacle.

When it was finished, God's glory filled the tabernacle like a cloud, and all the people could see that God was living among them.

Joshua Takes the Lead

Moses felt his old bones creaking as he climbed
Mount Nebo. From the top, he could see the
whole of Canaan, the land God had promised
to Abraham all those years ago. Moses had led
the Israelites for forty years, and now it was
time for someone else to take over.

Moses called his assistant, Joshua.

"God has chosen you to be the new leader of the Israelites," said Moses.

"Why me?" asked Joshua.

"You have always trusted God, even when things have been difficult or frightening," replied Moses.

Soon after, Moses died. Joshua was the leader now.

His first task was a tricky one. The Israelites needed to cross the deep, fast-flowing River Jordan.

Joshua made sure that the tabernacle was carefully packed up and reminded everyone that the ark of the covenant would go ahead of them.

"We don't know exactly where we're going," he said, "but God does."

The next day, the priests went first, carrying the ark of the covenant. The moment their feet

touched the water, the river stopped flowing.
The priests stood on the dry riverbed until
all the Israelites had crossed over. Then they
stepped out, and the water rushed back.

The Israelites were in Canaan at last.

The first place they reached was the city of
Jericho. Joshua looked at the high, stone walls
and the barred gates.

"How can we possibly get in?" he wondered.

But God told him what to do. "The priests must carry the ark of the covenant around the city once every morning for six days. On the seventh day, they must march around the city seven times while the priests blow trumpets. After that, get all the people to shout as loud as they can. Then watch what happens."

Joshua ordered the people to do exactly as God had said.

On the seventh day, the priests marched around seven times. Then all the people SHOUTED… and the city walls came crashing down.

The Israelites rushed into the city, and all the people in Canaan heard the amazing stories of what God had done.

With Joshua as their leader, the people of Israel were able to make their home in the land.

"Here we can all live as God's people should," declared Joshua.

Gideon Learns to Trust

A young Israelite called Gideon worked on his parents' farm in Canaan. It was a good land, but there was a big problem. The Midianites kept spoiling everything. They camped in the fields and trampled the crops; they stole food and animals.

Harvest time came, and Gideon needed to get the grain out of the wheat to make flour.

"I'll do it at night," he thought. "Then nobody can steal it."

As he was working, an angel appeared.

"God has chosen you to destroy the Midianites," declared the angel.

"Hmm…" Gideon scratched his head. "If what you're saying is true, then show me. I will take a clean, dry fleece from one of the sheep and put it on the ground. If, in the morning, the fleece is wet with dew and the ground is dry, I'll believe you."

Sure enough, in the morning, the fleece was wet and the ground was dry.

"Hmm…" Gideon rubbed his chin. "Just to be certain, I'll put another fleece out. This time, if the fleece is dry and the ground is wet, *then* I'll believe you."

It happened just as he had asked. Then Gideon believed that God wanted to help him destroy the Midianites.

Over the next few days, he gathered as many men as he could find – more than 30,000!

"Now *that's* what I call an army," said Gideon, proudly.

"There are too many men," said God. "Tell anyone who is frightened to go home."

Gideon did so, and most of the men left.

"There are still too many," said God. "Take them to the river to drink. Watch what they do."

   Most of the thirsty men knelt down and put
their faces close to the water.

   "An enemy could easily creep up on them,"
said God. "Send them home. Keep the ones
who scoop up the water in their hands."

   "But that only leaves me with 300!" cried
Gideon. "That's not enough!"

   "You don't need a big army," said God.
"You just need me."

One night, Gideon and his men crept to the Midianite camp. He split them up into three groups and gave each man a trumpet and a clay jar with a flaming torch inside.

Gideon's men tiptoed around the edge of the camp, and when Gideon blew his trumpet, they all yelled and trumpeted and smashed their jars so that flames flashed in the darkness.

The Midianites leaped up in a panic and in their confusion began to fight each other. Some were killed by the swords of their own men, and all the rest ran away in terror.

"Now we are free to live as God's people," announced Gideon. "We must worship our God faithfully."

For a while, everyone did as Gideon said, and all was well. Then the Israelites forgot about God and had to face a whole new group of enemies.

Samson the Strongman

Samson was the strongest man in Israel, strong enough to kill a lion with his bare hands. He used the strength God gave him to defend the Israelites against their enemies, the Philistines.

He set fire to their wheat fields; he picked up a bone and killed a thousand men with it. For twenty years he made trouble for them.

"We must get rid of Samson," they growled.

"But we can't capture him – he's too strong."

Now, Samson was in love with a Philistine woman called Delilah. She should have been his enemy, but he often stayed at her house.

The Philistine leaders went to Delilah. "We will reward you with silver if you find out how to take Samson's strength away," they said.

Delilah agreed to the plan.

One day she asked Samson, "What is the secret of your strength? Is there any way you could be tied up?"

"If someone ties me with seven fresh strips of leather, I'll be helpless," he said.

When Samson was asleep, the Philistines gave Delilah seven fresh strips of leather. She tied him up, then shouted, "Samson! The Philistines are attacking!"

Samson woke up and snapped the leather strips easily.

Delilah was angry. "You lied to me. You don't love me!" She pestered Samson so much that at last he told her the truth.

"It is God who makes me strong," he said.

"My long hair is a sign of a promise my mother and father made that makes me God's servant. If you cut my hair, I will be as weak as a newborn baby."

When Samson fell asleep, Delilah called a man to cut off Samson's hair. When he woke up, his strength was gone.

The Philistines captured him and put him in prison.

But Samson's hair began to grow.

One day, the Philistines were having a great celebration in the temple of their god. They took Samson there and chained him to two tall pillars.

Samson prayed to the real God. "Please let me have my strength, just one more time."

He pushed hard with both his arms, and the stone pillars gave way. The temple collapsed. Samson was killed, but so were all the Philistines with him.

Ruth's New Home

Two women trudged down the street in Bethlehem. The village people nudged each other.

"Look," said one. "Isn't that our old friend, Naomi?"

"But she left with her family years ago to live in another country," said another. "Why has she come back?"

"Naomi, where is your husband?" asked

the people. "Where are your two sons?"

"They are dead," said Naomi. "I have come home with my faithful daughter-in-law, Ruth."

Naomi and Ruth settled in Bethlehem. They had no money, but Ruth had an idea.

"There is a field of wheat near here," she said. "I will go and collect some of the leftovers."

Ruth went to the field and began to pick up grain from the ground.

The owner, Boaz, noticed her.

"I've heard all about you," he said. "You have been good to Naomi and stayed with her. You may gather as much as you like from my field."

Ruth went home with enough grain for a good meal, and plenty left over.

"Boaz is such a kind man!" she declared.

Ruth went back to the field often. Each time, Boaz made sure that his workers treated her well and left plenty of grain for her. Ruth and Naomi never went hungry.

But then the harvest ended. What would become of them now?

Naomi had an idea, and her eyes sparkled as she whispered it in Ruth's ear.

That evening, Ruth went to the place where
Boaz and his workers were sleeping. She crept
up to Boaz and lay down at his feet.

Boaz woke in the middle of the night and
jumped.

"Who are you?" he gasped, not recognizing
Ruth in the dark.

"It's me, Ruth. Will you marry me?"

When Boaz realized who it was, he covered her tenderly with the corner of his blanket.

"You don't need to worry any more," he said. "Go to sleep until morning."

So it was all arranged. Soon afterwards, Boaz married Ruth and they had a son named Obed. Naomi thanked God for giving her a family again.

Samuel Listens to God

Hannah had no children and longed for a baby. She prayed to God to send her a child.

"If you answer my prayer," she wept, "I will give the child back to you, to serve you all his life."

God did answer Hannah's prayer. She gave birth to a son and named him Samuel. 'When he was old enough, she took him to the place of worship, where the old tabernacle stood. There she handed him over to the old priest, Eli.

"God has given me a son," she said. "Now I'm offering him back to God."

So Eli looked after Samuel and taught him how to serve God. Samuel lived with Eli in the place of worship, and each year Hannah would bring him a new set of clothes.

One night, Samuel was in the tabernacle. He slept there most nights, to make sure the lamps burned safely. He was drifting off to sleep when a voice called him: "Samuel?"

"Here I am!" he said, jumping up. He ran to Eli. "You called me. Do you need something?"

"I didn't call you," said Eli. "Go back to bed."

But as Samuel tried to relax, the voice came again: "Samuel!"

"I'm not imagining it," thought Samuel. He got up and hurried to Eli. "You definitely called me this time. What do you want?"

"I did *not* call you," said Eli, angrily. "Go and lie down, boy!"

A third time the voice came: "Samuel!"

Samuel didn't want to make Eli angry, but what if he really *did* need something this time? He threw his covers back and went to Eli.

"You called me," Samuel said, wearily.

Eli realized that something unusual was going on. "This voice you heard – I think it must be God calling you," he said.

"God? Calling *me*?" Samuel couldn't believe it. He was just a boy. Nothing special. Why would the awesome God who had done so many miracles for the Israelites speak to *him*?

Eli nodded. "If the voice comes again, say, 'Speak, Lord, for your servant is listening.'"

Samuel scurried back to bed. He shivered a little and waited. Sure enough, the voice boomed: "Samuel! Samuel!"

"Speak, Lord," said Samuel, "for your servant is listening."

God gave Samuel a message for Eli, and from that moment on, Samuel listened carefully to what God had to say, then passed God's message on to other people.

A King for Israel

Samuel grew into a wise old man. He led Israel against their enemies and encouraged them to obey God. He hoped that one day, when he was gone, his sons would be good leaders after him. But they were dishonest and the people did not want them as leaders.

"We need a king to rule over us," they said. "All the other nations have one."

"God is your king," protested Samuel.

But the people insisted. "We want an earthly king too."

Samuel prayed to God about it, and God told him to choose a young man called Saul. Saul was tall and handsome but very shy. So shy that when Samuel wanted to show the people their new king, they couldn't find Saul anywhere!

God saw everything. He knew that Saul was hiding.

"Look behind the heap of sacks and bags," God said. "You'll find him there."

So the people brought Saul out and made him king, even though some people didn't think much of him.

"He'll be no good as a king," they grumbled.

But they were wrong. When their enemies were cruel to the Israelites, Saul was so angry that he defeated them all. Saul was a king to be proud of!

But Saul began to disobey God. He started to do things his own way instead.

"You have broken God's commands," Samuel told him, sadly. "God has chosen a new king – someone who will love God faithfully and lead Israel in the ways of God."

Samuel did not know who the new king would be. But God told him to go to a man called Jesse, who had eight sons.

"I will show you which one I have chosen," God told Samuel.

Jesse brought out his first son, who was handsome and strong.

"This must be the new king!" thought Samuel.

"No," said God. "It doesn't matter what he looks like. I'm more interested in what he's like inside. Loving me and obeying me are more important than looking good."

Jesse's next son came and stood before Samuel.

"No, it's not this one either," said God.

Samuel met seven of the sons, but none of them was the right man for the job.

"There's only the youngest one left," said Jesse. "David is out looking after the sheep."

"Go and get him," said Samuel.

As soon as David arrived, God said, "He is the one."

Samuel poured oil over David's head as a sign that he was set apart for a special task. God had chosen this young boy to be Israel's future king.

David and Goliath

One day, David's father sent him on an errand: to take some food to his older brothers, who fought in King Saul's army.

"I would be good at fighting," he thought. "I'm not afraid of anything."

When he reached the battlefield, David saw that King Saul's army had gathered on one side of a valley and their enemies, the Philistines, stood on the other.

As David greeted his brothers, one of the
Philistine soldiers stepped forward. He was
a giant of a man, and his spear was as big as a
small tree.

"That's Goliath," whispered David's brother.
"He comes out every morning and evening to
try and scare us."

Sure enough, Goliath roared, "Send someone to fight me if you think they're brave enough."

"I'll fight Goliath," said David.

Everyone roared with laughter, and someone ran to tell the king.

King Saul sent for David. "You're only a boy," he said. "You wouldn't stand a chance."

"I would," said David. "I've killed lions and bears when I was guarding my father's sheep. Please let me have a go. God will help me."

At last King Saul agreed. "But you must wear my armour," he said.

David tried on the armour, but it was so big and heavy that he could barely move. He wriggled out of it and picked up a big stick. He also took five smooth stones from the stream, to fit into his sling.

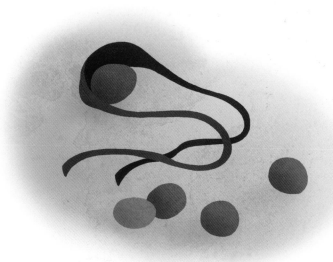

"I don't need anything else," said David. "God is on my side."

As David approached Goliath, the gigantic man began to call him names and laugh at him.

"Why do you have a stick?" he roared. "I am not a dog!"

David shrugged. "God has already won this battle," he said.

David put a stone into his sling, spun it around his head, and launched it straight at Goliath. It struck him on the head and knocked him to the ground!

"Now everyone knows that God is real and that he helps us," declared David.

David the King

King Saul frowned as he listened to the Israelites singing about David.

"David will want my kingdom next," he growled. "I will kill him."

But Saul's son, Jonathan, was great friends with David and helped him to escape. David hid in a cave, afraid for his life. Many times, Saul almost captured him, but David knew that God would take care of him.

"The Lord is my shepherd," he sang. "He will give me everything I need."

One day, a messenger came to David. He was filthy and his clothes were torn.

"What is it?" asked David. "What has happened?"

"Saul and Jonathan are dead. The Philistines killed them in battle."

David was terribly upset. He wept for both his enemy and his dearest friend.

"You are our king now," said some of the
Israelites, from the tribe of Judah.

But not everyone agreed.

"Saul has a son still alive!" they said. "He
should be the next king."

The argument grew into a war that lasted
several years. But David proved that he had
more courage and would make a better king.

This time, all the people of Israel agreed.

So David led his people to Jerusalem. He

defeated the people who were guarding it and took the city for his own.

"This is where we will worship God," he announced. "This city will be the centre of the kingdom."

David ordered that the ark of the covenant should be brought to Jerusalem. It was a day of celebration, with lots of music and dancing.

But David still missed his friend, Jonathan.

"Has he any family?" asked David. "I could do something kind for them."

The servants brought in a young man called Mephibosheth. He had something wrong with both his feet and found it hard to walk.

"This is Jonathan's son," they said.

From that day on, David treated Mephibosheth as his own son and allowed him to eat at the royal table with the rest of his family.

Life was good for David. He played his harp and sang songs of praise to God.

"I thank you, Lord, with all my heart, for your love and faithfulness."

David was brave, good, and kind. But
sometimes he did the wrong thing. One day,
he was on the roof of his house when he
noticed a beautiful woman washing herself.

"That's Bathsheba," his servants told him.
"She is married."

David wanted Bathsheba for his own, so he
sent her husband into a fierce battle, where he
was killed. David took Bathsheba to be his wife
instead.

After a while David began to feel terribly guilty. He knew that he had broken God's laws. He didn't eat or sleep.

"I have done the wrong thing," he cried. "Please forgive me."

"I do forgive you," said God, "but the things you have done will cause trouble in your family."

David changed his ways and obeyed God again. A little while later, he and Bathsheba had a baby boy. They called him Solomon.

Solomon Builds a Temple

When King David died, Solomon became king.

One day, two women came to him. They had a quarrel about a baby.

"It's mine," said one woman.

"No, it's mine!" said the other.

Solomon knew that one of them was lying. But how would he find out who was the real mother?

"Cut the baby in half," he said, "so that both women may have a piece of it."

"Fair enough," said the first woman. "Let's do it."

"No!" cried the second woman. "I'd rather give up the child than see it hurt."

Solomon knew then that the second woman was the real mother. She loved her child so much that she would do anything to keep it safe.

"Give that woman the baby," he said. "She is the real mother."

Then everyone knew that Solomon was the wisest man in the kingdom.

It was God who had made Solomon wise, and Solomon wanted to worship God properly.

"My father, David, wanted to build a Temple here in Jerusalem," he said. "I want a really beautiful building to replace the tabernacle."

Solomon's men worked for many years. They built a beautiful temple, glittering with gold, and a gleaming palace next to it.

In the Temple was a special holy room, where only the priests were allowed to go. The ark of the covenant was put into it, and a cloud of God's glory filled the Temple.

"I have made this Temple a special place for me and my people," God declared. "Solomon, if you love me and obey me, one of your family will always be king over Israel. But if you don't, I will take away from Israel this Temple and the land I have given them."

Solomon became so famous that even the rich
and beautiful Queen of Sheba heard about him.

"I will test him with difficult questions," she
said. "Then we will see how wise he is."

The queen arrived with lots of servants and
a string of camels carrying gold, jewels, and
expensive spices. She spent a long time talking
with Solomon and admiring his wonderful
palace. She realized that he was a great king
and gave him all the precious things she had
brought with her.

But as Solomon grew richer, things began to go wrong. He demanded more and more money from everyone; he forced people to do building work when they didn't want to. He had so many wives, he could barely count them – and they persuaded him that God wasn't the only true God. Solomon began to worship statues instead of the real God.

At last, Solomon grew old and died. His son Rehoboam became king. A man called Jeroboam spoke up for the people of the north.

"Your father forced us to work hard. He made life difficult for us. We will be loyal to you if you make things easier."

But Rehoboam replied, "You think my father made you work hard? I will make you work even harder!"

The people from the north were horrified.

"We won't do it," they said. "We don't want Rehoboam to be our king. Jeroboam would be much better."

So there was not one kingdom, but two.

Rehoboam was the king over the tribe of Judah, in Jerusalem.

Jeroboam was king over the rest of Israel. He didn't want the people to set foot in Jerusalem, so he set up his own places of worship. But the people of Israel worshipped statues instead of the one true God.

Rehoboam and Jeroboam fought with each other all the time, until they died.

After that, all the kings of Israel disobeyed God. And the worst of all was a king called Ahab.

Elijah and the Fire from Heaven

King Ahab told the people to worship a god called Baal. God was angry about this. He spoke to his faithful prophet Elijah, and Elijah passed the message on to Ahab.

"There will be no rain in this land unless I say so," announced Elijah.

Sure enough, no rain fell. The land dried up and the crops failed. Everyone was hungry.

God told Elijah to sit by a stream. Ravens brought him food and Elijah drank from the stream until it dried up.

"Now what?" he said.

God sent Elijah to the house of a widow and her son. They only had enough flour and oil for one last loaf of bread. But God promised that the flour and oil would never run out until the rain fell again. So everyone in the house was well fed.

In the third year of the drought, Elijah went to King Ahab.

"You need to worship God," he said. "Meet me on Mount Carmel with all the prophets of Baal, and God will show his power."

So Ahab gathered 450 prophets of Baal and they set up a contest to prove whose god was the most powerful.

The people of Israel watched as two piles of wood were heaped up; two bulls were killed and put on top of the wood.

"Now, call on Baal," said Elijah. "Ask him to send the fire to light the wood."

All 450 prophets of Baal called out to him. They shouted and danced around their woodpile from morning until evening. The noise was deafening. But there was no reply.

"Now it's my turn," said Elijah.

He poured water on his woodpile until it was dripping. He dug a trench around it and filled that with water too. Then he said one simple prayer: "Show them that you are God."

Instantly, the wood burst into flames. They were so hot and powerful that they not only burned up the wet wood and the bull, but the stones around it, the soil, and the water in the trench!

The prophets of Baal fell to their knees.

"Now we believe," the people cried. "Your God is the true and only God."

157

Naaman is Healed

Naaman lay on his bed, groaning. He was the commander of a great army, yet his worst enemy was the terrible skin disease that covered his body. His servant girl felt sorry for him, even though she was an Israelite and it was his enemy army that had captured her.

The girl was thoughtful as she combed the hair of Naaman's wife.

"If only my master would go to Elisha, the prophet from Israel," she murmured. "I'm sure he would be healed."

Naaman heard what the servant girl said. He had heard of Elisha, the prophet of God. Elisha had learned everything he knew from Elijah.

"I will go to Elisha's house," Naaman announced. "Prepare my chariot and horses!"

When Naaman arrived, he expected Elisha to
pray and put his hands on the diseased skin.
Naaman hoped he would be healed at once.

Instead, Elisha sent his servant to tell him to
go and wash seven times in the River Jordan.

"Nonsense! Why should I do that?" Naaman
was angry. "Why does it have to be the Jordan?
There are many rivers better than that one."

He went away in a rage.

His servants whispered together.

"You go and tell him," said one.

"No, you do it," said another.

At last, one of them was brave enough to speak to Naaman. "If Elisha had told you to do something really difficult in order to be healed, would you have done it?"

"Of course," snapped Naaman.

The servant gulped. "Then why not do this simple thing that he has asked you to do?"

Naaman was silent for a moment. At last he sighed.

"You're right. I will do it."

So Naaman went to the River Jordan, as Elisha had suggested. He stepped into the water, deeper and deeper until he was able

to duck right under the surface. Seven times he washed himself, and when he came out of the river, his skin was smooth and white. The disease had gone.

"I'm glad that I listened to that servant girl," thought Naaman. "She knew that the God of Israel could help me."

The Assyrian Army

King Hoshea ruled over Israel from the city
of Samaria. But he was a bad king and took no
notice of God's laws. When the king of Assyria
wanted to fight against him, Hoshea was afraid.

"Don't fight me," he begged. "I'll be your
servant and give you money each year."

But Hoshea was sneaky. He sent messengers
to Egypt to ask for help to fight the Assyrians.
And he didn't pay the money he had promised.

So the king of Assyria put Hoshea in prison.
He attacked Israel, captured Samaria, and
carried all the Israelites away to Assyria.

King Hezekiah ruled over Judah from the city of Jerusalem. He was a good king and obeyed God's laws.

The king of Assyria decided to attack Judah too. But King Hezekiah stood up to him and would not let him take Jerusalem.

Ten years later, there was a new king of Assyria. He decided that it was time to teach Hezekiah a lesson. So he sent his army to Jerusalem. Three of the most important men in the army brought a message. They stood outside the walls and shouted it, so that everyone could hear.

"Are you hoping that God will save you?" they said. "You might as well give up now. We've beaten everyone else. Come and join our side instead."

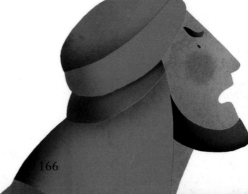

The king of Assyria also sent a boastful letter to King Hezekiah. *God can't help you*, it said. *He can't save your city of Jerusalem.*

King Hezekiah was so upset that he tore his clothes and went to the Temple, where he spread out the letter and prayed to God. God answered him by putting words in the mouth of the prophet Isaiah.

"Don't be afraid," said Isaiah. "God knows that you follow him.

"He will deal with the king of Assyria, and he will protect Jerusalem."

That night, God sent an angel to kill all the Assyrian soldiers, and the king of Assyria died soon afterwards.

Sadly, the kings of Judah who came after Hezekiah were wicked. God gave them many chances to return to him, but they ignored him every time.

Josiah and the Book of the Law

King Josiah looked out from his palace in Jerusalem, toward the Temple. He had only been eight years old when he became king of Judah, and his father and grandfather had been wicked kings.

But Josiah wanted to please God, as his great-grandfather, Hezekiah, had done.

Now he had grown into a young man and a good king.

Josiah called his servant. "Go to the Temple and see how much money we have collected. Share it out among the men who are working on the Temple. They will need it for repairs and materials."

It wasn't long before the servant came back. He seemed to be in a hurry and was so excited that he could barely speak. He was holding an old book.

"What have you got there?" asked Josiah.

"The priest found it in the Temple!" said the servant. "It's the book of God's laws!"

"The very commandments that God gave to his people?" Josiah gasped. "Read it to me!"

The servant read aloud everything that was in the book. As Josiah listened, he realized that, over the years, the people of Israel and Judah had turned away from God. They had chosen to do things their own way and they had broken all of the Ten Commandments.

Josiah was so upset that he cried and tore his clothes. "God must be so angry with us!" he said. "What will happen to us now?"

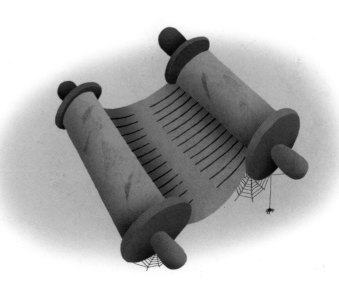

Josiah gathered all the people of Judah at the Temple and read the book of God's laws to them. They all agreed to follow God again.

Josiah went out into the land and got rid of everything that made God angry. He smashed up the statues of false gods; he chased away all the people who practised magic; he destroyed the places where people had done wicked things.

God said to Josiah, "Your grandfather was so wicked that the nation must be punished for the things he did. But you have a good heart, and it will not happen while you are still alive."

But one day, an Egyptian pharaoh killed King Josiah.

And that's when Judah's troubles really began.

Faraway Babylon

Jeremiah was a prophet. He wanted to warn the people of Judah. "You must change your ways, or God is going to bring disaster upon us! Tell him you're sorry, and follow him again."

But the people wouldn't listen.

The danger came from Babylon. The Babylonian king, Nebuchadnezzar, was very powerful. He had already invaded parts of

Egypt, and now he had his eye on Judah.

King Nebuchadnezzar ordered his soldiers to attack Jerusalem. They carried away all the treasures from the Temple and the palace. Worse still, they captured the people of Judah, including the king and his household. King Nebuchadnezzar sent his prisoners away to Babylon.

Only the poorest people were left behind.

"Who will lead us?" they whimpered.

"Stop complaining," said King Nebuchadnezzar. "I'll give you a king."

He chose a man who would do as he was told and gave him a Babylonian name, Zedekiah.

In spite of everything that had happened, Zedekiah did not ask God for help. Nor did he do as King Nebuchadnezzar had told him.

Things went from bad to worse.

King Nebuchadnezzar ordered his soldiers to surround Jerusalem so that nobody could go in or out. They sat outside the city for months. The farmers couldn't bring food in, so the people in Jerusalem began to starve.

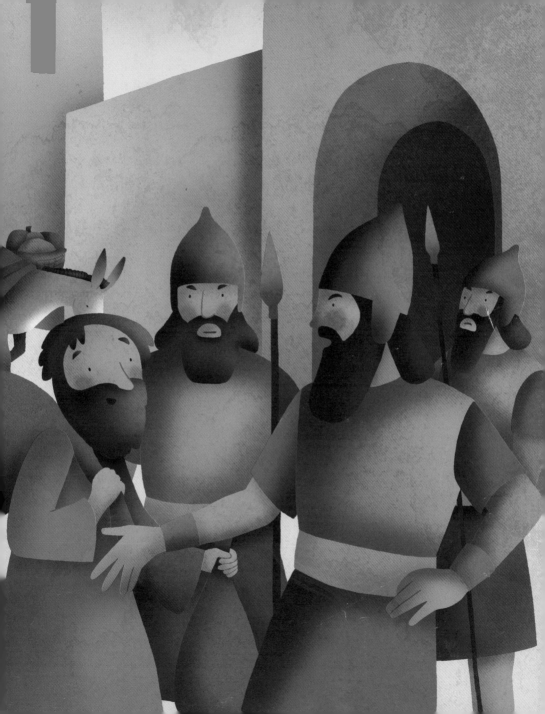

When everyone was too weak to fight, King Nebuchadnezzar's soldiers rushed into the city. They marched into the Temple and ripped out all the special things that were used for the worship of God. They even stole the ark of the covenant. The Temple was set on fire and the flames leaped to the sky, burning night and day until the Temple was gone. The soldiers burned the houses as well.

Jerusalem wasn't a proud city any longer; it was a smouldering scrap heap.

The people of Judah, now called Jews, had no
home of their own. They gathered by the river
of Babylon and cried. The Babylonians laughed
at them and tried to make them sing, but they
were too sad. They missed their home and were
sorry that they had abandoned God.

"But there is still hope!" said some.
"Remember what the prophets said."

The people gathered together often. They
listened while the priests reminded them of the
promises that God had spoken.

"Jeremiah said that God would take us home again after seventy years," said the priests. "And Micah promised us a new king, even better than David."

"A new king?" The people felt a flicker of hope.

"Yes. One day he will be born in Bethlehem, and he will bring us the peace and safety we long for."

The Fiery Furnace

When King Nebuchadnezzar captured the
Jews and brought them to Babylon, they found
themselves living in a strange place, far away
from home.

Among them were three young men.
Shadrach, Meshach, and Abednego were clever
and handsome. But they missed their home in
Judah. Here in Babylon, the food was different
and the language sounded strange.

King Nebuchadnezzar brought the young men to the palace to serve him. They learned to speak the language and how to live like Babylonians. They kept themselves healthy and studied hard.

"They are wiser than all my other servants," declared King Nebuchadnezzar.

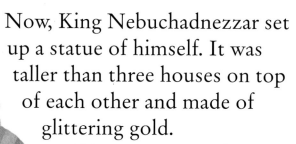

Now, King Nebuchadnezzar set up a statue of himself. It was taller than three houses on top of each other and made of glittering gold.

"Everyone must bow down to my statue and worship it," he ordered.

"If anyone doesn't, he will be thrown into a furnace of blazing fire!"

Shadrach, Meshach, and Abednego knew that even though they were far from their own country, they must only worship the one true God.

So they would not bow to the statue.

When King Nebuchadnezzar found out, he flew into a rage.

"Who do you think is going to save you?" he roared.

"God will save us," they said. "And even if he doesn't, we will still refuse to worship anyone else."

The king's guards tied them with ropes and took them to the fiery furnace. The flames were so hot that the guards were roasted as soon as they opened the door.

Meshach, Shadrach, and Abednego fell into the flames, but something very peculiar happened. King Nebuchadnezzar saw them walking around in the fire, free of their ropes!

"And who's that?" the king demanded. "We put three men into the furnace but there is a fourth... and that one looks like an angel."

The king went as close to the furnace as he dared and shouted, "Come out!"

Shadrach, Meshach, and Abednego stepped out of the flames. Their skin was not burned, their clothes were not blackened, and they didn't even smell of smoke.

King Nebuchadnezzar was astounded. "I shall make sure nobody ever says anything bad about God again!" he said.

Daniel and the Lions

Daniel was another young Jewish man brought
to Babylon, where he served the kings faithfully
for many years. But Babylonia's enemy, Persia,
was too powerful. At last the Persian king,
Darius, sat on the throne and ruled over the
land.

Daniel served him equally well. In fact, King Darius was so pleased with Daniel that he planned to put him in charge of the entire kingdom. The other servants and officials were jealous. They tried to get Daniel into trouble, but they couldn't find a single thing to complain about.

"He's always such a *good* man," they muttered. "We'll never catch him out unless we use the laws of his God to trap him."

So they came up with a plan. They went to the king, bowing to hide their sly smiles.

"You are the king," they declared. "Everyone should come to you with their prayers and requests. They shouldn't pray to anyone else."

"What a good idea!" said King Darius. "And what shall happen to anyone who disobeys?"

"Throw him to the lions," cackled the officials.

So King Darius declared a law throughout the kingdom that everyone must pray to him and no one else.

But Daniel still prayed to God.

The servants scurried to the king. "Daniel is praying to God!" they shouted. "Throw him to the lions!"

The king liked Daniel, but he couldn't change the law. Sadly, he ordered that Daniel must be taken to the lions' den.

The lions paced up and down hungrily, growling and licking their lips.

"I hope your God will rescue you!" said King Darius, and he shut Daniel in.

The king tossed and turned in his bed all night, fretting over his friend. As soon as it got light, he hurried to the lions' den.

"Daniel? Are you…?" He gulped. "Are you there?"

There was a moment of silence.

Then came Daniel's voice. "Yes, I'm fine! God sent an angel to help me, and the lions didn't even dare to lick me."

King Darius was thrilled that Daniel was safe.

"Your God is the true God," said King Darius, "and his power will go on for ever!"

Esther:
Queen for a Reason

"There is to be a contest! The king is looking for a new queen!"

The news spread throughout Persia as King Xerxes sent out his servants to find every beautiful young woman in the land.

One of them was a Jewish girl, Esther, who lived with her cousin, Mordecai. She was taken with the other girls to the palace, where they were pampered and preened for a whole year. Then the king chose his favourite – it was Esther!

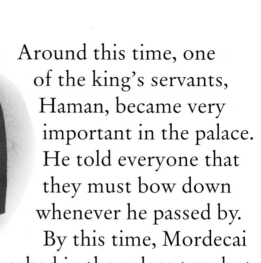

Around this time, one
of the king's servants,
Haman, became very
important in the palace.
He told everyone that
they must bow down
whenever he passed by.
By this time, Mordecai
worked in the palace too, but
he refused to bow down to Haman,
so Haman became very angry.

"Who is this man?" he growled. "Is
he a Jew? Then let's kill him. No, wait!
Let's kill *all* the Jews!"

Haman went to King Xerxes and
whispered all kinds of lies about the Jews. "You
must destroy them," he sneered.

King Xerxes gave Haman permission to
deal with the Jews however he wanted. So
Haman gave the order that on a certain day,
every Jew in the land was to be killed. All
over the country, the Jews wept and wailed,

remembering the days when they had loved God and lived safely in their own land.

Mordecai told Esther of the king's order. "You must go to the king and beg him to change his mind."

"But I am only allowed to see the king when he calls me," said Esther. "If I go and see him myself, he will probably kill me."

"If you don't go, then you will die anyway, for you are Jewish too," said Mordecai. "But Esther, just think – what if God arranged for you to be the queen at this time, just so that you may be able to help his people?"

"Then pray for me!" begged Esther. "Gather all the Jews in the city and call on God for three days!"

Brave Esther went to King Xerxes, and he was so pleased to see her that he welcomed her.

Queen Esther threw a banquet for the king, with rich foods and wine. Haman was her special guest. But while they were feasting, Esther told King Xerxes everything that Haman had done, and how he had planned for all the Jews to die. The king was angry, and he went outside to think. When he came back in, Haman had hold of Queen Esther and was begging for his life.

"How dare you attack my queen in her own palace?" roared the king. "Take your hands off her. You shall die for this!"

And so Haman was killed next morning, and, thanks to Esther's bravery and God's forward planning, the Jews were safe once more.

Return to Jerusalem

After the Jews had been in Babylon for seventy years, God made the king of Persia feel sorry for them.

"You've spent enough time away from your home land," he declared. "You can go back!"

Not all the Jews wanted to go. By this time, they were quite happy in Babylon, with homes

and families and businesses. But some did decide to go back.

When they got there, Jerusalem was in ruins. But the people thanked God for bringing them back – "God's love for us goes on and on," they sang. "He has brought us home at last!"

They began to rebuild the Temple. The people who lived there were angry that they were not allowed to join in, and they tried to upset the building plans. But the Jews didn't give up, and at last, after years of hard work, the Temple was finished.

Then the people quickly forgot about God's love and his laws, and they went back to the wicked old ways that had caused all their problems in the first place!

A priest called Ezra came back to Jerusalem, to make sure that everything was done properly in the Temple. He was horrified to see what was going on.

"You must change your ways!" he said. "Get rid of everything and everyone that stops you loving God properly."

Another man, Nehemiah, came back to rebuild the city walls. It was a huge job, but everyone worked together to build different parts of the wall. Enemies tried to stop the building, and the men had to keep hold of their weapons while they worked.

"I don't think we can do it," moaned some of the workers. "It's all too difficult and dangerous."

"Nonsense," said Nehemiah. "Remember that God is great and awesome."

Eventually the walls were completed and the doors fitted. Jerusalem was safe again, and the Temple was inside.

Ezra gathered all the people together in the city square and read God's words to them – all the stories of the wonderful things God had done, of his love and patience, of his wonderful promises.

"God is so amazing," cried the Jews. "We are sorry that we have hurt him by turning away. We want to belong to him again."

"Then don't be upset," said Ezra. "Let's have a party!"

All the people went out into the countryside and gathered branches and leaves. They built shelters for themselves to remember when Moses had led them through the desert. They ate and drank delicious things, and held the biggest celebration ever!

God had never given up on them.

God had brought them home.

Jonah Runs Away

Some of the Jews found it hard to do as Ezra said. He told them they should not marry people who weren't Jews.

"Why not?" asked the people. "Does that mean God doesn't care about other nations?"

But of course, God did love and care for everyone. The story of Jonah helped them understand.

Jonah was a man who tried to run away from God. "Go to Nineveh!" God had told him, but Jonah was too scared to go there. Instead, he got on board a ship.

"I'm *not* going to Nineveh," he muttered as his ship sailed away from the harbour. "Our enemies, the Assyrians, live there, and they are cruel and terrifying. This ship will take me far away and God won't ask me again."

A massive storm blew up and tossed the ship about so much that it threatened to fall apart.

Jonah looked at the towering waves and gulped. "This is my fault. I'm running away from God, and he doesn't like it. It's not fair that everyone should die because of me. Throw me overboard!"

"No way!" cried the sailors. They did their best to row to safety, but the storm was too wild. "We're sorry," they cried, their voices like gulls above the howling wind. And they tipped Jonah into the sea.

Down and down went Jonah, through the dim green depths.

But God sent an enormous fish with a gaping mouth to scoop Jonah up and carry him around the ocean for three days.

At last the fish spat Jonah onto the beach.

"*Now* will you go to Nineveh, as I asked you?" said God.

Jonah couldn't say no again. He went to Nineveh and gave them the message God had told him: *If you don't change your ways and say sorry to God, he will destroy your city.*

The king of Nineveh was horrified. He ordered the people to stop doing wicked things at once and to obey God.

God knew they were sorry.

"I will not destroy them after all," God said.

"*What?*" shouted Jonah. "I came all this way to give them your message, and you're going to let them off?" He stomped off in a rage to sit outside the city.

The sun was scorching and Jonah was sweating, so God made a tall plant grow. Jonah lay back and relaxed in its cool shadow.

Next morning, God made the plant shrivel up, and Jonah's skin began to burn in the sweltering heat.

Jonah stood up and shook his fist at God. "Now I am *really* angry!"

"But don't you see?" God said. "Just as you wanted the plant to live, I wanted the people of Nineveh to live. I love to forgive people, no matter what country they come from or what bad things they have done."

THE NEW TESTAMENT

A New King is Born

Mary hummed as she swept the floor. She was thinking about Joseph, the man she was going to marry.

All of a sudden, someone spoke. Mary jumped. There was an angel in the corner of the room! "You're going to have a baby," said the angel.

"Name him Jesus. He will be the Son of God, the new king the Jews have been waiting for."

Mary was amazed. How could she have a baby? She wasn't married yet. But sure enough, as the months passed, she grew big with a baby.

Joseph took care of her, even though he wasn't the baby's real father – God was!

Then came more surprising news. "The Roman emperor wants everyone to go to their home town to be counted," Joseph told her. "We have to go to Bethlehem."

"But it's almost time for the baby to be born!" said Mary.

"The donkey will carry you," said Joseph.

The journey to Bethlehem was long and bumpy. By the time they got there, Mary was exhausted. She was looking forward to a comfortable bed and some food. But all the inns were full. There was nowhere to stay.

At last, an innkeeper took pity on them.

"I have a stable," he said. "It could do with a clean, but it's warm and dry."

Mary was glad to sit down on a pile of straw. The baby came quickly after that, with a loud cry as it gulped in air.

"It's a boy," said Mary, "just as the angel told us. His name is Jesus."

She wrapped Jesus tenderly in strips of cloth. She shooed the donkey away from the manger and laid the baby in it.

Out in the fields, a group of shepherds huddled around their fire. One was dozing; another two were talking quietly.

Suddenly, the sky seemed to explode with light. The shepherds screamed and hid their faces.

There was an angel speaking to them!

"Don't be scared," said the angel. "I have

good news, which will bring joy to all people, everywhere. The king that God promised has been born at last, in Bethlehem. He's lying in a manger, wrapped in strips of cloth."

The sky grew even brighter as thousands more angels appeared, singing for joy.

All at once, they were gone. Only the stars glimmered silently in the darkness.

One of the shepherds jumped up. "What are we waiting for? Let's go to Bethlehem and see this baby!"

They each scooped up a lamb and raced off to the village. They hammered on doors, they called out in the streets, and at last, in a scruffy stable, they found Mary and Joseph gazing down at their baby, Jesus.

"What we saw was amazing!" gabbled the shepherds. "The angel said…" They told Mary what had happened, the words tumbling off their tongues.

And Jesus slept on, smiling in his sleep as the echo of the angels' song still whispered on the air.

A Visit from the Wise Men

King Herod scowled at his messenger. "I don't want any more visitors."

"But they are wise men from the east. They are looking for a new baby king."

"There is no baby here," snarled Herod, "but I suppose I must deal with them. You had better show them in."

The wise men looked tired and dusty, as though they had come a long way. But there was a look of excitement in their eyes.

"We have studied the stars for many years," they said. "A new, bright star has appeared. It means that the king the Jews have been waiting for has been born at last. Where is he? We want to worship him."

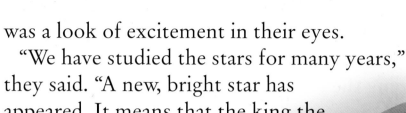

Herod was worried. He didn't want a new king taking his throne!

"Go and look for him, then come and tell me where to find him," said Herod. "I'd like to worship him, too."

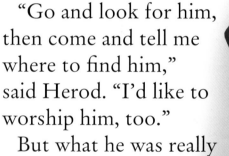

But what he was really thinking was, "I'll kill that wretched baby."

So the wise men continued on their journey. The star seemed to move across the sky, leading them onward. At last it stopped over Bethlehem.

The kings halted their camels.

"That's the place," they said.

Sure enough, they went into the town and found Mary, Joseph, and Jesus.

They knelt down and unwrapped the gifts they had brought – strange things to give to a baby.

"I've brought gold," said one of the wise men, "because he is a king."

"I've brought frankincense," said another, opening a pot. "It burns with a scent that reminds us of God."

"And I've brought myrrh," said a third. "It's used to prepare bodies after death. There will be sadness and suffering in Jesus' life."

"What about King Herod?" they said to each other. "Shouldn't we go and tell him the baby is here?"

"No!" One of the wise men spoke up. "I had a dream last night, and it warned me not to go back to Herod."

So the wise men climbed onto their camels and went back to their own country a different way.

After they had gone, Joseph had a dream, too: a very bad dream, in which an angel warned him that Herod was coming to kill Jesus.

Joseph got up, even though it was the middle of the night, and woke Mary.

"We must leave at once!" he said.

And the family fled through the darkness, to Egypt, where Jesus would be safe.

Jesus Grows Up

Jesus was the Son of God, but he grew up in the village of Nazareth as an ordinary boy in an ordinary family. He learned woodwork from Joseph and played games with his friends. He went to school at the synagogue and grew up learning the stories of the Jews.

When Jesus was twelve years old, his parents took him to Jerusalem to celebrate the feast of the Passover. Jesus loved to hear the amazing story of how God had brought his people out of Egypt. He enjoyed eating the bread that reminded him of that special night. During the days of the feast, he spent hours in the Temple, listening to the older men talk about God.

Mary and Joseph set off back to Nazareth among a crowd of friends. Children darted in and out, chasing one another or tagging along with other families.

At the end of the day, Mary turned to Joseph. "Have you seen Jesus today? Do you know who he's walking with?"

Joseph shrugged. "He's probably with his cousins."

Mary and Joseph asked everyone they knew, "Is Jesus with you?" But he was nowhere to be found.

Mary went pale. "We must have left him behind!"

"Don't worry," said Joseph. "He's twelve years old, almost a young man. He'll be fine." But as they turned back, he broke into a run.

For three anxious days, Mary and Joseph searched all over Jerusalem. They looked in inns, gardens, and market places; they looked in the wild areas where he might play.

At last they went into the Temple, and there
was Jesus, listening intently to the Jewish
teachers.

"What do you think you're doing?" Mary's
voice came out angry, but she hugged Jesus
tightly. "We were so worried about you!"

Jesus frowned. "But didn't you know where
I was? This is my Father's house. It's where I
belong."

Jesus went back to Nazareth with his parents and did as they asked him. But he knew that life held something different for him. He was, after all, no ordinary boy.

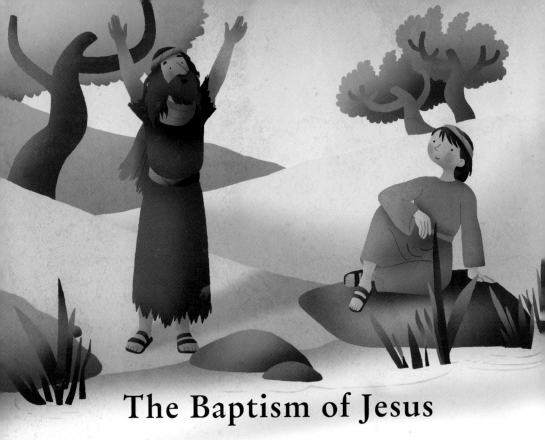

The Baptism of Jesus

Jesus had a cousin called John, who spent his life teaching people about God.

"Get ready!" John said to the crowds. "Someone special is coming, sent from God as part of his plan from the very beginning. You must change your ways and say sorry to God for the wrong things you have done. God calls them sins, and they stick to you like dirt."

Many people were sorry, and to show that they were making a fresh start, John baptized them in the River Jordan.

John prayed for each person and lowered them into the river. "Just as the water cleans you, so God has washed your sins away," he declared.

But someone else was there that day. Someone very special indeed.

Jesus, grown into a man.

John gasped. "There he is!" he shouted. "The one I've been telling you about!"

Jesus said, "I want you to baptize me, too."

"But you don't need to be washed clean!" said John.

"Baptism is the right start for me," replied Jesus.

So John and Jesus stepped down into the river. John lowered Jesus below the water and then raised him again. The moment Jesus came up, the sky seemed to roll back. The Spirit of God came down in the form of a dove, and settled on Jesus.

A voice came from heaven, more powerful and beautiful than the rushing waters of the river: "This is my Son. I love him and I am very pleased with him."

The Holy Spirit led Jesus into the nearby
desert. Jesus knew that God had some very
important things for him to do, and he spent
forty days praying. During that time he ate no
food, so that he could concentrate completely
on God.

The devil came to him and whispered, "If you
really are the Son of God, you can turn these
stones into bread. Go on – they will fill your
hungry belly."

"God has said that people don't only live on bread," said Jesus. "They also need to listen to God's words."

The devil kept trying to make Jesus turn away from God. But it was no use.

He could not fight against God's powerful words. He gave up and went away. Jesus had beaten him.

Follow Me

Jesus was ready to begin the work God wanted him to do. But he needed a few special friends to help him.

One day, Jesus was by Lake Galilee when he noticed two brothers, Simon and Andrew, hauling nets into their fishing boat.

Jesus called out to them, "Follow me, and I will show you how to catch people instead of fish."

The brothers came to shore. They knew about Jesus and all the amazing things he did. They followed him straight away.

A little farther on, two more brothers were sitting mending their nets. Their names were James and John.

"Follow me," said Jesus.

James and John jumped up, left behind their boat, and went after Jesus too. They weren't going to miss out on an adventure!

Jesus did seem to like calling people away from their work. Matthew collected tax money from the Jews to give to the Romans. He was sitting at his stall, counting money, when Jesus came along.

"Follow me," said Jesus.

Matthew was so excited to be chosen by Jesus that he threw a huge party and invited all his friends – other tax collectors and people who weren't liked because they didn't follow God's laws.

The Jewish teachers in the synagogue were horrified when they saw Jesus enjoying himself and making new friends at these parties.

"Why on earth are you mixing with people like those?" they sniffed.

"God has sent me to them because they need me," replied Jesus. "Besides, I like them!"

In the end, Jesus chose twelve men to be his disciples. Their names were: Simon (also known as Peter), Andrew, James, John, Philip, Bartholomew, Matthew, Thomas, another James (who was younger), Thaddaeus (sometimes called Judas), another Simon, and Judas Iscariot.

These twelve men – and many other men and women who wanted to learn from Jesus – went with him everywhere, learning about God and helping him to teach and heal people.

The Lord's Prayer

The disciples noticed that Jesus spent time
every day praying to God.

"Will you teach us to pray?" they asked.

"All you need is this simple prayer," replied
Jesus.

"Our Father in heaven:
May your holy name be honoured;
may your Kingdom come;
may your will be done on earth as it is in heaven.
Give us today the food we need.
Forgive us the wrongs we have done,
as we forgive the wrongs that others have done
to us.
Do not bring us to hard testing,
But keep us safe from the Evil One."

Jesus the Teacher

Hundreds of people began to follow Jesus
around, eager to hear what he might say next.
He began to teach everyone about how God
wanted them to live.

"You already know that you mustn't kill
anyone," said Jesus, "but being angry with
someone for no reason is just as bad. It makes
God sad when you do these things."

Some people began to wriggle uncomfortably. How could they be as good as God wanted them to be?

"It's easy to love your friends and the people who live the same way that you do," said Jesus, "but God wants you to love your enemies as well."

"Love your *enemies*?" People nudged one another and whispered behind their hands. This wasn't what they had expected to hear.

"And you don't need to worry about anything," continued Jesus.

Some of the people frowned. They had families to take care of, homes to build. They always needed food and clothing.

"Flowers don't have to work for their beautiful petals," said Jesus, pointing at the countryside. "And God makes sure that birds have plenty to eat." A bird flew overhead, a berry in its beak. "If you stop worrying about all these things and think about being part of God's kingdom instead, God will make sure you have everything you need."

The people looked at one another. "Does God really care about us that much?" they said.

Jesus smiled and told them a story.

"A man built a house on
rocky ground. He made sure the foundations
were strong.

"Another man built a house nearby, on sandy
ground. He hurried his work, stuffing holes
with straw and slapping mud over the cracks.

"Soon afterwards, a storm rushed in. The rain
turned the ground into a swamp.

"The house on the rock was perfectly safe,
but the house on the sand gave a great *creak*

and collapsed in a heap."

Some people in the crowd roared with laughter; others thought about their own houses and looked worried.

"It's a great story," they said, "but what does it mean?"

"If you listen to all the things I teach you, and do as I say," said Jesus, "you will be safe and secure when life gets difficult."

The Sower and the Seeds

One day, Jesus told a new story.
"A farmer went out to sow many, many
seeds."
The people in the crowd nodded.
They had seen the way farmers
walked up and down, tossing handfuls
of seeds in every direction so that all
the soil was covered.
"As the farmer was scattering
the seeds," Jesus went on,
"some fell on the path.

"People and animals walked on them, and hungry birds swooped down and pecked them up. Those seeds never even started to grow.

"Some of the seeds fell on rocky ground. They put out tiny roots and leaves, and began to grow. But there was no water for them because the rock was hard, so these baby plants shrivelled up and died.

"Some of the seeds fell into a patch of thorns. The seeds began well, but the thorns grew even faster. They took all the light and the water, and they strangled the farmer's plants until they turned brown and died as well."

The crowd began to murmur. What an unlucky farmer! His family would surely go hungry.

"But..." continued Jesus, "some of the seeds

fell onto good, rich soil. They sprouted and grew strong. They produced a marvellous crop for the farmer!"

The people thought this was a good story, but the disciples knew that it must have a special meaning.

"Please explain it," they begged.

So Jesus did. "The seeds are like my message that God loves everyone and wants them to be part of his family.

"Some people don't believe it; they are like the seeds on the path.

"Some people believe for a while, but when things get difficult, they give up.

"Others believe the message. They begin to love God. But their worries and problems grow like thorns, and they stop believing."

Jesus looked sad at this, but soon he smiled again.

"Some people believe my message with all their heart. They follow me and love God and become part of his family for ever."

Jesus Forgives and Heals

The four friends puffed and panted as they struggled through the streets, carrying a man on a mattress.

"It would be much easier if you could walk!" joked one of them.

"That's not likely to happen, is it?" sighed the man, looking down at his legs, which didn't work properly.

When they reached the house where Jesus was, they tried to push through the crowd, but the doorway was crammed with people. So the four friends heaved the mattress up the outer stairs and onto the roof.

They began to dig. They burrowed through the layers of reeds, mud, and chalky plaster to make a mattress-sized gap between the wooden beams.

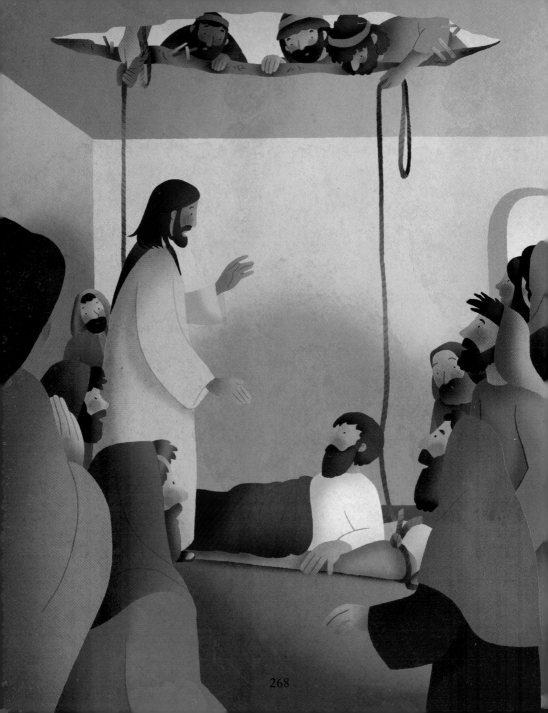

They took hold of the ropes they had tied at each corner of the mattress and lowered the man through the roof.

He saw the look of amazement on people's faces as he came to rest right at the feet of Jesus. His own face burned with embarrassment, but he forgot all that when Jesus looked at him.

"Your friends have such faith!" exclaimed Jesus. "My friend, your sins are forgiven."

"How like Jesus to know what the real problem was," said the man to himself. He had wrong thoughts in his mind that caused him far more trouble than his helpless legs. Now Jesus had set him free! His heart filled with joy.

But the Jewish teachers, who had come from all over the land to hear what Jesus had to say, were horrified.

"You can't say that," they shouted. "It's outrageous! Only God can forgive sins!"

Jesus nodded. "And to prove that I *do* have that power, watch this." He held out a hand to the man. "Get up and walk," he said.

The man's legs began to tingle. They twitched and itched as the strength began to return. Could he really do it?

He reached out and took hold of Jesus' hand, and staggered to his feet.

"I can stand!" he cried. "I can walk! Praise God!"

Sailing Through the Storm

Wherever Jesus and his disciples went, crowds followed them, and by the end of the day, they were exhausted.

One evening, they were standing by Lake Galilee.

"Let's sail over to the other side," suggested Jesus.

The disciples knew all about boats, so they

worked and chatted while Jesus crawled into
a comfortable space where the ropes and nets
were stored. He found something to rest his
head on and settled down to sleep.

As the night wore on, heavy clouds gathered.
"I think there's a storm coming," said Peter.
The other disciples knew the wild storms that
whipped the lake into a mass of churning water.
They didn't want to be out in it.

They gripped the sides of the boat. "Will we
reach the other side before it hits us?"

Peter's answer was lost in the rising wind.
The disciples tried to haul in the sails, but the
gale yanked them free.

"Tie down anything that's loose!" shouted
Peter as the waves slapped the boat.

Crack! A deafening boom of thunder ripped
the sky open, and needles of rain stabbed the
disciples' skin. The waves became mountains;

the wind became a siren; the disciples' fingers
slipped on the knots and the boat groaned like
a falling tree.

Jesus slept on.

"Jesus! WAKE UP!" yelled the disciples.
"Don't you care that we're all about to
drown?"

Jesus opened his eyes and squinted at the sky.
He yawned, stretched, and stood up.

"Be quiet!" he said to the wind. The wailing
stopped, and the flapping sails hung loose.

"Be still!" he said to the waves. They fell back
and stopped pawing at the boat.

The disciples collapsed in a heap, gasping and
wiping wet hair from their eyes.

"Why do you get so scared?" asked Jesus.
"Don't you believe that God can protect you?"
At these words, the disciples became
frightened all over again.
"Who is Jesus *really*?" they whispered.
"Look! He can control the weather, and only
God can do that."

The Girl Who Came
Back to Life

Jostling and pushing, shoving and shouting:
Jesus and his disciples were caught in the
middle of yet another crowd.

But Jesus noticed one person in particular:
Jairus. He was a respectable Jewish leader, but
he had a problem that couldn't be fixed by
keeping laws and celebrating festivals. Only
one person could help.

"Jesus!" called Jairus, nudging people aside with his elbows. "I need your help!"

He knelt down at Jesus' feet.

The crowd muttered to one another. "He's such an important man. Why is he kneeling in the dirt?"

"My daughter is ill. I'm afraid… I'm afraid…" Jairus could hardly get the words out. "I'm afraid she's going to die."

Jesus crouched and put a hand on Jairus'
shoulder. "Don't be afraid," he said. "Get up
and take me to your house."

Jairus got up and hurried home, with Jesus
close behind.

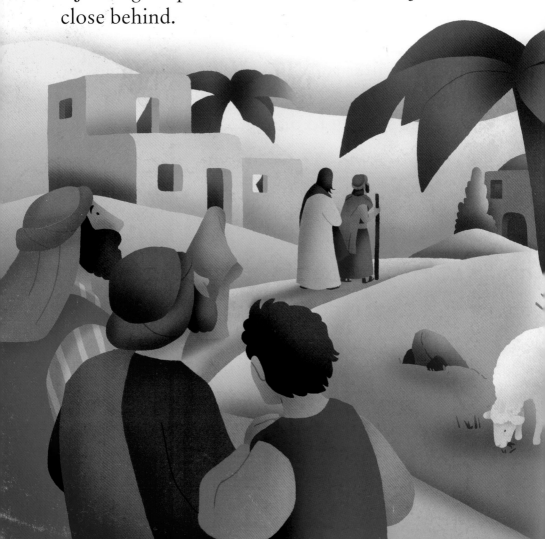

"We can't miss this!" said the people in the crowd, so they followed too.

A messenger came running.

"It's too late!" he wailed. "The girl is dead. Jesus can't do anything now."

But Jesus looked into Jairus' eyes. "Don't be afraid," he repeated. "Just keep on believing that I can help."

When they reached Jairus' house, it was full of people sighing and sobbing.

"What's all this fuss about?" said Jesus. "The girl is not dead; she's only sleeping."

"Nonsense!" they said. "She's definitely dead."

Jesus ordered them all to leave the house except the girl's parents and three of his disciples.

He went into the room where the girl's body lay, still and silent, on the bed. He took her small hand in his strong one and whispered, "Little girl, get up!"

The girl's eyelids fluttered. She took a deep breath. She sat up and looked around.

"She's alive!" gasped Jairus, and he grabbed her to him in a huge hug. "Thank you, Jesus. You even have power over death!"

The Perfect Picnic

One day, the people found it so interesting listening to Jesus that they stayed late into the evening. A small boy in the crowd opened his bundle of food and licked his lips. Five barley loaves and two delicious salty fish. It was long past mealtime, and he was starving.

A shadow fell over the boy. He looked up. There stood one of Jesus' disciples: it was Andrew, and he looked tired.

"Excuse me," Andrew said. "Would you be willing to share your food?"

"Who with?" said the boy.

"Everyone," said a familiar voice. Jesus stepped forward.

"But my little meal won't be enough," stammered the boy.

"It will be if you give it to me," said Jesus.

The boy handed over his food. It would have been so nice to taste even a little bit of it, but he couldn't say no to Jesus.

Jesus said a prayer of thanks and handed the
boy some bread and a piece of fish. Then he
gave the same to a woman sitting nearby. And
the same again to her child.

Jesus handed bread and fish to his disciples,
and they began to pass the food among the
crowd. The boy watched as Jesus changed his
small meal into a feast for everyone.

The boy ate and ate. Five chunks of bread, six
and even seven. Four delicious handfuls of salty

fish. When everyone in the crowd had eaten
their fill, the disciples collected the leftovers in
twelve big baskets.

A man rubbed his tummy and lifted a hand
in thanks to Jesus. "I don't know about you,"
he said to the boy, "but that's what I call a
miracle!"

The boy smiled, licking the last piece of bread
from his lips. "And that's what *I* call a perfect
picnic!"

The Runaway Son

"Once there was a man who had two sons," began Jesus. "The younger son couldn't wait for his father to die so that he could have his share of the house and the money. 'I want it now!' he said.

"The father was sad, but he let the boy make his own choices. The son went far away and spent all the money doing exactly as he pleased.

"But money doesn't last for ever, and soon it was all gone. The son had no food, no friends, and nowhere to live. He took a job looking after pigs and he was so hungry that he was tempted to eat the smelly pig food.

" 'I'll go home,' he thought. 'I'll tell Father how sorry I am.'

"All this time, the father had been thinking about his son, hoping that he might come home, and watching the road day after day. One day, he glimpsed a small figure trudging along in the distance.

"The father leaped up, gathered his robes above his ankles, and raced to meet his son. He hugged him and couldn't bear to let go.

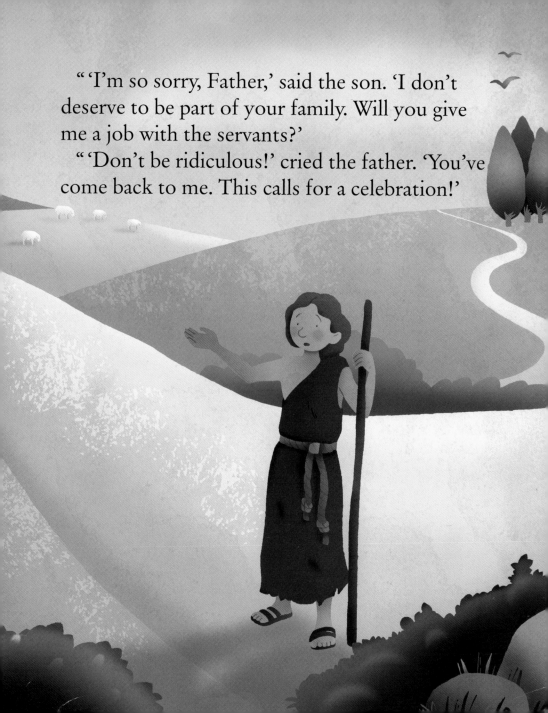

" 'I'm so sorry, Father,' said the son. 'I don't deserve to be part of your family. Will you give me a job with the servants?'

" 'Don't be ridiculous!' cried the father. 'You've come back to me. This calls for a celebration!'

"The father threw a huge party and all the bad things the son had done were forgiven.

"But the elder son was angry. 'I'm not coming,' he growled. 'How can you celebrate like this after everything he has done? You've never thrown a party for me!'

The father hugged his elder son. 'I am so happy that my lost son has come back home,' he explained. 'And I love you just as much. I always have and I always will. I share with you everything I own.' "

When Jesus finished the story, the people were quiet for a while. They knew that Jesus was trying to show them how much God loved them, like the father in the story.

The Lost Sheep

Sometimes Jesus felt sorry for the crowds of people that followed him about. He knew that they had worries and problems, and he wanted them to know how much God cared for them.

"They are like sheep without a shepherd," he thought, and he began to tell them a new story. "Once there was a shepherd who had a hundred sheep."

Some of the children in the crowd tried to count to a hundred, but they soon ran out of fingers to count with. "One day," Jesus continued, "the shepherd was checking that all his sheep were safe and healthy when he discovered that one of them was missing."

The children gasped.

"Maybe a wolf caught it!" shouted one.
"Or perhaps it fell down a hole," called
another.

Jesus nodded. "The shepherd was worried, so he left the ninety-ninety sheep grazing peacefully and set off to look for the missing one.

"He searched all day long. He looked behind every bush, every rock, and every tree. He peeked in every cave, every hole, and every valley.

"At last, tired and thirsty, the shepherd heard the lost sheep bleating."

Some of the children gulped. Would the shepherd be angry with the sheep for running away?

But they didn't need to worry.

"The shepherd lifted the sheep and put it on his

shoulders," said Jesus. "He was so thrilled to find his sheep that he carried it all the way back home and had a party with his friends.

"There is a celebration like this in heaven when one person says sorry to God and becomes part of his family."

A Wedding... and a Helpful Stranger

Jesus loved to celebrate life with people. He went to weddings and funerals, feasts and parties.

"Imagine a wedding," he began, "and all the preparations that must be done – food, drink, music, special clothes, invitations…"

People in the crowd nodded. They knew all about these!

"Now imagine a wedding where there were ten bridesmaids."

The people knew that the bridesmaids' job was to wait until the bridegroom arrived, then light their lamps and show him into the wedding ceremony. The bridesmaids never knew exactly when he would come.

"That evening, the bridegroom took such a long time to arrive that the bridesmaids fell asleep!" said Jesus.

"At midnight, there was a loud shout from the bridegroom's friends. He had arrived! He needed the lamplight.

"The ten bridesmaids woke up. Five of them were well prepared and held up brightly glowing lamps. But the other five hadn't planned on such a long wait. Their lamps had been burning all this time, and they had run out of oil.

"They hurried away to buy or borrow more oil, but while they were gone, the bridegroom's party and the five wise bridesmaids went into the wedding.

"When the five foolish bridesmaids returned, they were locked out of the party."

Locked out? The crowd were shocked. How terrible to miss the celebration and be left outside in the dark!

"Everyone is invited to be part of God's kingdom," explained Jesus, "but some people just aren't ready."

"What do we need to do?" asked one of the Jewish teachers.

"Love God, and love other people," replied Jesus.

"Which people?" asked the teacher.

In answer, Jesus began another story.

"A man went on a journey from Jerusalem to Jericho," he said.

The people shuddered. That was a dangerous road!

"On the way, some robbers jumped on him, beat him up, and left him in the road. A priest came along the road and saw the man. Did he stop to help? No, he did not.

"Then another Temple worker passed by. Did he stop to help? No, he did not.

"At last, a stranger from Samaria came by. Did he stop to help?"

"No," booed the people. Jews did not like people from Samaria.

"Yes, he did," said Jesus. "He cleaned and bandaged the man's wounds. Then he put the man onto his donkey, took him to an inn, and paid the innkeeper to take care of him."

"What?" The people couldn't believe it.

"So who showed love in this story?" asked Jesus.

The people had to admit that it was the helpful stranger.

"This is how you must treat everyone, whether you like them or not," said Jesus.

Zacchaeus Changes
His Ways

It was a nuisance being so short. Zacchaeus was stuck at the back of the crowd and couldn't see a thing. A massive man stood in front of him, blocking the view.

Zacchaeus poked the man in the back. "Get out of the way!"

The man turned around and folded his big, beefy arms.

"Get out of the way yourself," he snarled. "Nobody wants you around. Go back to your house and count all the money you've taken from us."

"But I want to see Jesus!" said Zacchaeus.

"Jesus won't want to see *you*," said the man.

The man was right, thought Zacchaeus. *And yet…* Zacchaeus had heard stories about Jesus. He cared for people that were often ignored. He welcomed noisy children and enjoyed their company. He healed people that nobody else wanted to go near. He even made friends with tax collectors.

Jesus noticed people in a way that nobody else did.

Suddenly someone shouted, "Jesus is coming!"

Zacchaeus squeezed between the elbows
that blocked his way and ran ahead of everyone
to the road. But there were still too many
people. He couldn't see a thing!

A tree stood nearby, with a branch that
Zacchaeus could reach. He grabbed hold of it
and heaved himself up. He climbed high among
the leaves, ignoring the scrape of bark against
his shins.

No sooner had Zacchaeus settled himself in
the tree than Jesus came walking right beneath
him. Zacchaeus had a great view of the top of
his head!

Jesus stopped. He looked up.

"Ah, there you are, Zacchaeus," he said.

Zacchaeus was so shocked that he almost fell
out of the tree. Jesus knew his name!

"Come down," said Jesus. "I want to come to
your house."

"*My* house?" stammered Zacchaeus. "Why?"

"I want to eat with you."

Zacchaeus slithered down and walked home with Jesus, listening carefully as Jesus talked with him.

"Why has Jesus gone with *him*?" grumbled the crowd. "Perhaps Jesus isn't the good person we thought he was."

But their fears turned to cheers when Jesus and Zacchaeus returned.

"I'm going to give back all the money I've stolen," declared Zacchaeus. "In fact, I'll give back four times as much."

Jesus smiled. "That's why I came," he said; "to find the people who are lost and to bring them into God's kingdom."

Jesus and the Children

There were always plenty of children in the crowds around Jesus. Sometimes they sat and listened; sometimes they raced in and out of the tall adults, giggling and shrieking.

One boy jumped up to chase after a stray cat.

"Oh no, you don't." His mother grabbed his arm. "I want Jesus to bless you. Come on."

The boy pulled away. But then he noticed that other parents in the crowd were taking their children forward, too. He felt suddenly shy and excited at the same time. He had heard Jesus telling stories, of course – some of them funny, some of them a bit frightening, but all somehow impossible to forget. But Jesus was so important! He wouldn't want to waste his time on a child, would he?

The disciples seemed to agree.

"You can't bring children through," they said, barring the way with their strong fishermen's arms. "Jesus is busy enough as it is."

Jesus looked up. He stared straight at the boy, and his eyes were kind.

"Bring the children here," he ordered. "Never try and keep them away from me. God's kingdom belongs to them. In fact, everyone should believe in me the same way these children do."

He smiled, laid his hands on the boy's head, and blessed him.

Jesus in Jerusalem

Jesus and his disciples were on their way to
Jerusalem. Jesus had been saying some strange
things. He seemed to think that he was going
to be killed, but then he would come back to
life again!

The disciples were puzzled, but they went with him, whispering and worrying all the way.

When they reached a village near the edge of the city, Jesus sent two disciples ahead.

"You'll find a young donkey tied up," he said. "No one has ever ridden it. I'd like you to untie it and bring it here. Tell anyone who asks that the Lord needs it."

A little while later, there was the thud of hooves in the dust and the two disciples returned, leading a young donkey.

The donkey had no saddle, so the disciples laid their cloaks across it for Jesus to sit on. As he rode into the city, people lined the streets, waving palm branches and shouting for joy.

"Blessed is the king who comes in the name of the Lord!" they sang, and they lay their cloaks on the road to make a royal carpet beneath the donkey's hooves.

Once he was inside the city, Jesus went to the Temple. He remembered God's words to Solomon hundreds of years before: this was God's house, where people of any language or country could come and pray.

Now it was more like a marketplace. Stray cats darted in and out of the stalls where cooing doves were being sold for high prices. The people who came to make their festival offering to God were being cheated out of their last coins.

Anger rose in Jesus. "People should not have to pay to come and worship my Father!" he roared. "This is *God's* house, and you have made it a den of robbers!"

Amid a flurry of wings and shouting, Jesus began to overturn the stalls.

"Nobody should stop people from coming to God," he declared.

From the shadows, the Jewish leaders watched. They nodded to one another and began to make their plans to get rid of Jesus.

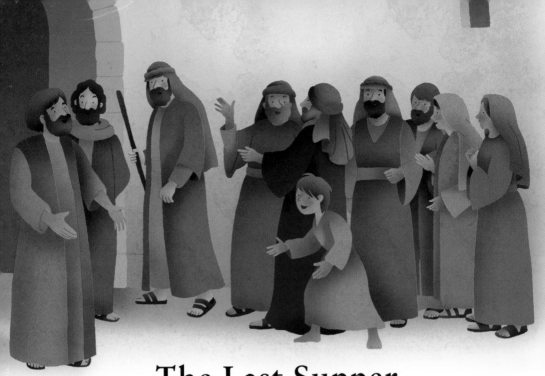

The Last Supper

Jerusalem was crammed with people, talking and laughing, jostling and tripping over one another. It was the Passover celebration, the time when the Jews thanked God for bringing his people out of Egypt all those years before.

Jesus and his disciples were among the crowds. They almost had to shout to make themselves heard.

"We need somewhere to have our special

Passover supper," said Peter, rubbing his stomach as he thought of the roast lamb they would eat.

"Yes – where shall we have it?" asked John.

"It's all arranged," said Jesus. "You will meet a man carrying a jar of water. He will show you a large upstairs room where you can prepare everything."

It all happened as Jesus had said, and by the time night fell, he and his twelve disciples were gathered around the low table, ready to eat.

Jesus picked up some of the flat bread. He thanked God for it and broke it in two, then shared it out among them. "This is my body, given for you," he said as he gave each disciple a piece.

The disciples looked at one another, shrugged, and ate the bread. Why was Jesus talking in this strange way again?

Then Jesus took a cup of wine. "This is my blood, given for you," he said. "God is

beginning a new covenant with all people."

The disciples shifted uncomfortably. Was Jesus really going to die? But that was unthinkable! He had come to be the king of the Jews, hadn't he? If he died, everything they believed in would be over.

"But one of you will betray me," said Jesus, looking at the disciple named Judas Iscariot.

Judas hurried away. Had Jesus found out about his plan?

When the meal was finished, Jesus went out to a garden called Gethsemane. His disciples went with him.

"Pray for me," whispered Jesus, his face anxious.

He moved away to talk to God on his own. His face was pale and he began to sweat.

"*Please*, Father," he begged. "Don't make me suffer. Please find an easier way for me. But if it's what you want, then I will do it."

While he was still praying, there was a commotion at the entrance to the garden. Torchlight glinted on spears; rough voices rang out in the darkness.

It was a band of soldiers, looking around at
Jesus and the disciples.

"Which one is it?" muttered one of them.

Judas Iscariot was with them. He stepped
forward and kissed Jesus on the cheek.

"That's the signal!" said the soldier. "He's the
one!"

The soldiers stepped forward, shoving Judas
aside and grabbing hold of Jesus.

They took Jesus to the Jewish leaders, who
asked him if he was indeed the Son of God.

"I am," Jesus replied. The leaders were shocked.

No one was allowed to say that! It was against their laws.

"This man must die," they said.

Jesus knew that he could call on thousands of angels to help him, but he also knew that the most important task of all lay ahead.

The First Easter

The Jewish leaders took Jesus to the Roman leader, Pontius Pilate.

Pilate questioned him and at last declared, "He hasn't done anything wrong."

"He's a troublemaker," growled the leaders.

Pilate sighed. "Send him to the ruler of Galilee and let him decide what to do."

When the ruler saw Jesus standing before him, he rubbed his hands.

"Show me a miracle!" he demanded, and he pestered Jesus with lots of questions.

Jesus said nothing; he did nothing. The ruler and his soldiers made fun of Jesus and called him names. They dressed him in a royal robe for a joke and sent him back to Pilate.

"I'm going to let him go," announced Pilate.

"No!" roared the crowd, full of Jewish leaders. "Crucify him!"

"Crucify him? Nail him to a cross?" thought Pilate. "But that is the worst death for the worst kind of criminal."

But the crowd kept on shouting and Pilate didn't want to upset them. So he agreed.

The soldiers took Jesus away. They whipped him and spat on him; they twisted a crown out of spiky thorns and pressed it onto his head.

Then Jesus was nailed to a cross.

His mother, Mary, was there, watching and weeping. John, Jesus' disciple, put his arms around her.

"Let John be your son now," said Jesus, gritting his teeth against the pain. "John, take care of Mary as though she were your own mother."

All Friday afternoon Jesus hung there, and at last he died.

Some of Jesus' followers took his body down, wrapped it in cloths, and took it to a garden. They laid it in a cave tomb, rolled a heavy stone across the entrance, and went home, numb with shock and sadness.

Early on Sunday morning, one of Jesus' women followers, Mary Magdalene, went to the tomb. She was horrified to see that the stone over the doorway had been rolled back, and that the tomb was empty. She raced back to the disciples.

"Jesus' body has gone!" she sobbed. "Someone must have stolen it!"

Peter and John hurried back with her and went into the tomb.

"Look at the cloths," breathed John. "They are still here, as though the body has just vanished out of them in one piece!"

Peter and John ran off, back to their homes, to tell the other disciples what had happened.

Mary stayed behind, still crying. She didn't understand.

She looked into the tomb again, and saw two angels sitting where Jesus' body had been.

"Why are you crying?" they asked.

"Someone has taken Jesus away, and I don't know where they've put him," said Mary.

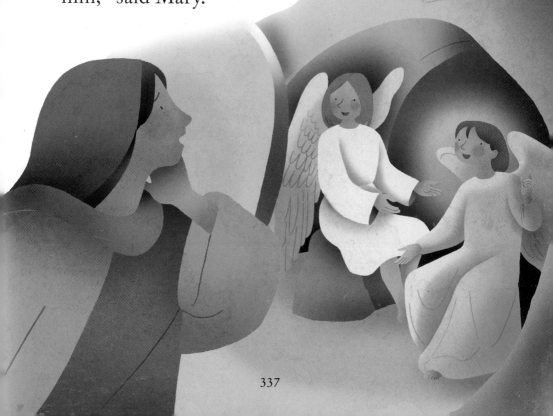

All at once, she realized there was someone behind her. She turned, her eyes blurred with tears. A man was standing nearby. "Oh! You must be the gardener," she began.

"Why are you crying?" he asked. "Who are you looking for?"

"Have you put Jesus somewhere else?" Mary wept. "If you have, please tell me. I just want to see him."

The man spoke a single word: "*Mary.*"

In that moment, Mary recognized both the voice and the man.

"It *can't* be…" she gasped.

But it was. Jesus himself stood there. He was alive!

Alive Again!

On Sunday evening, the disciples were huddled together in one room.

"The Jewish leaders might want to kill us too," said one of them. "Lock the door!"

After the doors had been locked, Jesus appeared in the room.

The disciples gasped and shrank back in fear.

"Peace be with you!" said Jesus.

He held out his hands, where the nails had

made holes. He showed them the wound in his side, where the soldiers had stabbed him.

"It really *is* you," said the stunned disciples.

Then they erupted into shouts and cheers, hugging Jesus and one another, crying with joy and astonishment.

Jesus laughed. "Peace be with you!" he said again.

But Thomas was not with them, and by the
time he returned, Jesus had gone. Thomas
listened to everything the disciples told him,
but he just couldn't believe it.

"Dead bodies don't just jump up again," he
said. "I have to see Jesus for myself, to put my
fingers on his scars. Then I will know it's true."

A week later, Jesus appeared in the room again.

"I'm glad you're here, Thomas," said Jesus. "Come and have a close look at my wounds. Touch them if you like, to see that they're real."

Thomas saw Jesus; he heard Jesus speak; he touched the wounds in Jesus' hands. There was no doubt about it.

Jesus had come back from the dead. He really was alive!

The Promised Gift

Over the next forty days, Jesus appeared to the disciples and other people many times.

"Don't leave Jerusalem," Jesus told his disciples. "Wait for the gift my Father promised."

"Gift? What gift?" The disciples were puzzled.

"You will receive power when the Holy Spirit comes on you," promised Jesus.

Power? The disciples liked the sound of that! Mostly, they didn't feel very powerful. They felt a bit scared and mixed up.

"You will tell people about me and everything you have seen me do," said Jesus. "You will tell people in Jerusalem, out into the countryside of Judea, and even in Samaria."

"That's not all," Jesus went on. "You will tell people from all over the world! I will always be with you, to the very end of time."

After he had said this, Jesus was taken up into heaven. The disciples watched, astonished, as he disappeared into a layer of cloud. They were still staring upwards when two angels appeared, dressed in dazzling white.

"Why are you still standing here, looking at the sky?" they asked. "Jesus will come back one day."

The disciples went back to Jerusalem and tried to wait patiently for the gift Jesus had promised.

On the festival day of Pentecost, the house
they were in was filled by a strange, wild
sound, like the howling of a gale. Something
like flames rested on the head of each disciple,
without burning them. Suddenly, the disciples
were able to speak in many different languages.

Jews from different countries had gathered in
Jerusalem for the festival. When they heard the
commotion, they were astonished.

"Aren't these people fishermen from Galilee?"
they asked. "They're not usually very clever.

How can they have learned all these different languages?"

Every Jew heard the story of Jesus in his own language. Peter stood up and explained what was going on. They were so amazed at what they heard that many of them believed in Jesus and were baptized at once; 3000 more followers joined the disciples that day.

The Church Begins

All the believers, old and new, were so excited about Jesus' message that they spent most of their time learning about it, talking about it, and praying. They met together every day, sharing meals and all their possessions.

Full of the power of the Holy Spirit, the disciples even did miracles, just like Jesus had done.

"Remember what Jesus said?" Peter asked John one day as they were going to the Temple for afternoon prayers. "He promised that we would be able to do all the things he did, and more."

John grinned. "It's not us doing it, though. It's God working through us."

As they neared the Temple, a man was sitting by the gates. He had never been able to walk and had to beg for money.

"Spare a coin?" he called out as Peter and John came closer.

Peter looked at him. "I don't have any silver or gold, but I have something better to give you. In the name of Jesus Christ of Nazareth... *walk!*"

Peter grasped the man's hand and pulled him up. At once, the man's feet straightened and his ankles became strong.

"So this is what it feels like to walk!" he said, and he followed them into the Temple, walking and leaping about, praising God at the top of his voice.

Saul: a Changed Man

More and more people heard the message
of Jesus and believed it. People called them
"Christians" after their leader, Jesus Christ.
  One of them, Stephen, went around
performing miracles and telling people that
Jesus had risen from the dead.

"He's a troublemaker. We must get rid of him," growled the Jewish leaders.

They dragged him out of the city and hurled rocks at him, while a young man called Saul held their coats.

Saul hated the Christians.

"They say that people can't please God just by keeping laws," he growled. "They say that God forgives anyone who asks – including people who aren't Jews."

Saul went from town to town, seeking out Christians and making sure they were punished, or even killed.

One day, Saul was on his way to Damascus to arrest some Christians. When he was nearly there, a dazzling light from heaven flashed around him. Saul fell onto the ground and a voice rang out:

"Saul, Saul. Why are you trying to hurt me?"

"Wh… who are you, my Lord?" stammered Saul.

"I am Jesus," said the voice. "When you hurt my people, you hurt me. Now get up and go into the city."

Saul staggered to his feet, lost for words. He was blind, and his men had to lead him into the city.

Three days later, God spoke to one of the
Christians, a man called Ananias.

"Go to a house on Straight Street," God told
him. "Saul is there, praying."

"*Saul*?" Ananias trembled at the name. "He
hates us!"

But Ananias trusted God. He went to the
house on Straight Street, took a deep breath,
and went in.

He passed on God's message. "Jesus has sent me to you," he said. "He wants to make you see clearly and to fill you with the Holy Spirit."

Ananias laid his hands on Saul, and something like fish scales fell from Saul's eyes. He could see again!

"Now I know that Jesus is real and alive," said Saul. "Please baptize me at once."

From that moment on, Saul was a changed man.

Paul Suffers for His Faith

Saul gave up his whole life to tell people about Jesus. He began where he was, in Damascus. First, he spent a few days with the disciples, learning as much as he could from them. Then he went straight out and began to speak in the synagogue.

"This is all very odd!" said the people who heard him. "Is this the same Saul that killed Christians? Now he's talking like them!"

But Saul used all his learning to prove to them that Jesus was the one promised by God from the beginning, who would come and save all people, whether they were Jews or not.

The Jews in Damascus were angry, and they plotted to kill Saul. They hid near the city gates and watched closely, waiting to pounce on him when he left to go back to Jerusalem. But one night Saul's friends hid him in a basket and lowered it through an opening in the city wall. He landed outside the wall and was able to escape in the dark.

During the next few months and years, Saul changed his name to Paul and journeyed to different countries to tell people about Jesus. He healed people and even brought a young man back from the dead – all in the name of Jesus.

But Paul faced danger around every corner.
   In one city, he and his friend Silas were
arrested for speaking about Jesus. Soldiers
whipped them and put them in a cell right in
the middle of the prison, with chains around
their ankles and a guard to watch them closely.
   Paul was not downhearted. Instead, he and

Silas spent the night singing praises to God.

Around midnight, an earthquake shook the prison so hard that all the cell doors sprang open and the chains of all the prisoners fell off! The man in charge of the prison was so amazed that he believed in Jesus and was baptized.

In other cities, Paul was whipped and put in prison again. People wanted to kill him by throwing stones at him, just as he had done to the Christians in the past.

The time came when Paul was a prisoner yet again, and he was sent to Rome. He boarded a ship with other prisoners. Soldiers guarded them, and the captain made plans to set sail. But Paul knew the seas in that part of the world. He knew that it was the time for storms and dangerous waves.

"Let's wait a while," he said to the captain. "You may lose your ship and we will all die!"

But the captain wouldn't listen.

Before long, a gale blew up and battered
the ship so badly that the crew had to tie it
together with ropes to stop it breaking up.

   After two whole weeks, the storm was still
raging. The ship drew near land and crashed
onto a sandbank.

"Kill the prisoners!" yelled the soldiers. "Otherwise they will swim away and escape!"

But the army officer wanted to keep Paul alive.

"Everyone into the water!" he shouted. "Swim for your lives!"

Some managed to swim; others clung to pieces of wood. And every single person got safely to shore.

Paul's life was tough, but he thought it was all worth it – to know Jesus.

A New Heaven and a New Earth

Sometimes life was hard for the Christians. Other people did not agree with their beliefs and did not want to hear the amazing truth that Jesus was alive for ever. The Christians suffered for their faith.

But they remembered that Jesus had promised to come back one day.

"When people don't expect it," they reminded each other, "Jesus will return to the earth and take all his people to be with him for ever."

Paul encouraged everyone by writing letters about this. "Even the people who have already died will come back to life, just as Jesus did," he told them. "God will give them a new, special body that will never get tired or ill."

Another Christian called John described what life would be like in this wonderful future.

"God will make a new heaven and a new earth," he wrote. "They will be one place, and everything will be perfect. There will be no crying, and nobody will be angry or upset.

"There will be a beautiful city made of precious jewels, with streets of pure gold and a sparkling river. And by the river will stand the Tree of Life – the same one that God planted in the garden when the earth was first made.

"This time people who love God will be allowed to eat its fruit and live with him for ever. Nothing will ever separate people from God again."

Word List

If you would like to know what these words mean, remember to look up the full story and read it. That will help you to understand better. The page numbers tell you which story to look at first, but you might find the same word in later stories, too.

angel a heavenly messenger from God 24

ark a ship 26

  a special box 88

Babylon an ancient city by a river 176

banquet a special meal for lots of guests 201

baptism/baptize to dip a person in water, showing that they want to live God's way 240

betray to turn against someone 325

bless/blessing ask for God's love and protection 46

Canaan the land that God promised would belong to his people 39

celebration a joyful party 110

Christ a name given to Jesus, meaning "Chosen One" 354

commandments laws 84

covenant a promise that cannot be broken 88

daughter-in-law the wife of your son 113

disciples people who follow Jesus and learn to be like him 250

disobey choose to do the wrong thing 127

drought a time of no rain, when everything is dry 154

faith complete trust 269

forgive stop feeling angry with a person about something they did 143

frankincense gum from a tree, burned to make a sweet smell 230

funeral a time when people gather to mourn a dead person 298

furnace an extremely hot oven 184

glory the magnificent presence of God 90

harvest when crops are gathered for food 64

heaven where God lives and rules 50

holy dedicated to God 147

Holy Spirit the invisible form of God, working
  in the world 244

inn a place for travellers to eat and sleep 222

Israel/Israelites all the people that came from the twelve
  sons of Jacob 70, 71

Jerusalem the holy city of Jewish people 138

Jews people who came from the kingdom of Judah.
  Jesus was one of the Jewish people 182

locusts grasshopper-like insects that eat crops 80

manger a feeding trough for animals 222

Midianites enemies of Israel 98

miracle an amazing event that only God can do 287

myrrh preserving spice, often used to prepare a dead
  body for burial 230

sheaves bundles of wheat or grain tied together 58

Sinai the mountain where God spoke to his people 86

sins things that people do that hurt other people and God 240

slave someone who has to work for no money 62

sling a weapon made from a strip of leather 133

synagogue a place where Jewish people meet 234

tabernacle a special tent where God met with his people before there was a Temple 90

temple a special building where people go to worship God or their god 110

tomb a cave where a dead body was put 334

tradition something that has been done the same way for a long time 53

widow a woman whose husband has died 153

worship adoring God 119

yeast something that makes bread rise 83

Index